WILLIAMS
SONOMA
———
CALIFORNIA

At Home

FAVORITES

110+ Recipes from the Test Kitchen

Happy Cooking!
xxx
Belle

RECIPES BY
**WILLIAMS SONOMA
TEST KITCHEN**

weldon**owen**

CONTENTS

INTRODUCTION

Welcome to the second edition of Test Kitchen favorites, a collection of recipes we like so much that we knew we had to bind them into a book to put on our shelf and, hopefully, on yours.

Connection is at the core of what we do—connecting with friends and family over a meal, connecting with strangers on the Internet over the best recipe for chocolate chip cookies or roast chicken, connecting with our childhood memories of a grandmother's apple pie or a father's pasta sauce, and connecting with past generations who instilled the love of cooking. Love is also central to what we do. Whether for an ingredient, a cooking method or tool, a friend who shared a dish, or the feeling you experience when sitting down to a simple, delicious meal, love has also helped to inspire this book.

In the following pages, you will discover scores of our favorite recipes. They are the ones we regularly make for ourselves and for our families and friends. Some are old, deciphered from nearly illegible scribbles in culinary-school notebooks or pulled from the pages of cookbooks that defined our earlier years. Others are a result of a phone call to a family member to ask for the recipe for a childhood birthday cake or for the secret to cooking a whole fish Chinese-style. Still others are new, based on our own imaginations or on a memorable meal we had in our travels to countries all over the world. And some are a combination of all these influences.

This collection also reflects how each of us cooks. Belle's cooking is rooted in nostalgia-fueled comfort food but with modern twists that keep your palate guessing. Devon centers her cuisine on a true Californian's pursuit of the freshest local ingredients and on achieving the well-balanced bite. And Lena takes on global cuisines, introducing spice and heat and flavor combinations that spark both interest and excitement.

Although we each have our own style and food personality, when it comes to recipe requirements, we share the same four focuses. First, we have learned that the integrity of an ingredient—from fruits, vegetables, and meats to dairy, oils, vinegars, spices, grains, and more—can make or break a recipe, so every ingredient must be selected with care. Second, flavor is complex and wildly subjective, and while we all have our own likes and dislikes, the foundation of flavor comes down to one thing: balance. To master flavor in any dish, you must focus on at least two of the five pillars of flavor—sweet, salty, sour, bitter, and umami—to ensure they coexist harmoniously—in other words, to ensure they are balanced. Third, the old saying that we eat with our eyes first is overused but true. A successfully presented dish sparks excitement before the first bite, and while for the most part our presentation style in the Test Kitchen is casual and cool, we are always careful to reflect the cook and/or origin of the dish and to include contrasting textures and colors.

And lastly, our fourth focus is on the pleasure of cooking. Williams Sonoma founder Chuck Williams once said, "My life's purpose has remained the same since the moment Williams Sonoma opened: to share with others the pleasure of cooking." We strive to do the same—to provide not only the inspiration to tackle that intimidating baking project or the tools to make cooking tasks easier but also the tips and tricks we have learned along the way to make cooking for yourself, your friends, and your family a pleasure.

Belle, Devon & Lena

ENTERTAINING WITH TEST KITCHEN FAVORITES

Brunches, bashes, barbecues—we at the Test Kitchen love a good get-together. Many of these recipes are designed with friends in mind, so if you're thinking of entertaining but don't know where to start, we've got you covered. Here are seven menus for seven very different types of gathering, from a relaxed family supper to a romantic date night.

BRUNCHING WITH FRIENDS

La Dolce Vita Spritz

Farmers' Market Frittata

Poppy Seed Popovers with Smoked Salmon and Crème Fraîche

The Test Kitchen Chopped Salad

THE LAST-MINUTE DINNER PARTY

The Ultimate Roast Chicken

Bucatini al Limone

Wild Mushrooms with White Wine and Thyme Butter

Fresh Salad Greens with Shallot-Dijon Vinaigrette

Last-Minute Fruit Cake

DATE NIGHT

New York, NY, Spicy Rigatoni

Belle's Pan-Seared Ribeye Steaks with Rosemary and Garlic, Family-Style

Rich Chocolate Mousse

Your Favorite Bottle of Cabernet Sauvignon

PLANT-BASED FEAST

Fresh Basil Mezcal Margarita

Mushroom Burgers with Dijon Aioli and Pickled Red Onions

Smashed Cucumbers with Mustard Vinaigrette

Oven-Baked Rosemary-Parmesan Fries with Three Dips

Devon's Puffed Quinoa Chocolate Crunch Bar

FAMILY SUNDAY SUPPER

English Family Lasagna

Roasted Broccoli Caesar with Corn Nuts

Swirled Summer Pesto Focaccia

Skillet Chocolate Chip Cookie

DRESS TO IMPRESS

Cheese-Stuffed Fried Squash Blossoms

Balsamic Braised Short Ribs

Classic Parmesan Risotto

Basque Cheesecake with Salted Brandy-Caramel Sauce

ALFRESCO SUMMER

Concha's Guacamole

Steak Cobb Salad

Tomato and Garlic Confit with Whipped Ricotta and Toasted Sourdough

Sunken Blueberry Cake with Mascarpone Whipped Cream

COCKTAILS & OTHER THIRST QUENCHERS

We call blackberries the "best berry" in the Test Kitchen. And combining them with bourbon to create our version of the classic Kentucky Buck takes them to a whole new level. You can make this as an individual cocktail, but for a party, nothing beats a pitcher of this flavorful punch.

THE PUNCH

SINGLE COCKTAIL SERVES 1

3 fresh blackberries, plus 1 for garnish

1 fl oz (30 ml) simple syrup, homemade (page 213) or purchased

2 fl oz (60 ml) bourbon

¾ fl oz (20 ml) fresh lemon juice

2 dashes Angostura bitters

3 fl oz (90 ml) ginger beer, chilled

Fresh mint sprig, for garnish

In a cocktail shaker, add the 3 blackberries and the simple syrup, then gently muddle together. Add the bourbon, lemon juice, and bitters, then fill with ice. Cover and shake vigorously until chilled.

Fill a highball glass with ice, then double strain the cocktail into the glass. Top with the ginger beer. Garnish with a blackberry and mint sprig. Serve immediately.

BATCH COCKTAIL SERVES 5

1½ cups (6 oz/170 g) fresh blackberries

⅔ cup (5 fl oz/150 ml) simple syrup (page 213)

1¼ cups (10 fl oz/300 ml) bourbon

½ cup (4 fl oz/120 ml) fresh lemon juice (from about 3 large lemons)

10 dashes Angostura bitters

2 cans (each 7½ fl oz/225 ml) ginger beer, chilled

Fresh mint sprigs, for garnish

Fill a large pitcher half full with ice. Set aside. In a cocktail shaker, add half the blackberries and the simple syrup, then gently muddle together. Add half the bourbon and all of the lemon juice. Cover and shake vigorously until chilled. Strain into the pitcher with ice.

Add the remaining bourbon and the bitters to the pitcher. Stir for 10–15 seconds. Top with the ginger beer and stir again. Garnish with the remaining blackberries and the mint sprigs. Serve immediately.

Inspired by one of our favorite traditional Mexican cocktails, the Paloma, we introduce a floral note with the addition of St-Germain, an elderflower liqueur whose natural sweetness replaces simple syrup in the recipe. The sugary salted rim is optional, but we think it looks really pretty and is the perfect nod to this cocktail's origin.

ELDERFLOWER PALOMA

MAKES 1 COCKTAIL

1 tablespoon kosher salt

2 tablespoons sugar

1 grapefruit wedge

4 fl oz (120 ml) fresh grapefruit juice

2 fl oz (60 ml) tequila blanco

1 fl oz (30 ml) elderflower liqueur, preferably St-Germain

3 dashes Angostura bitters

Grapefruit sparkling water or plain sparkling water

3-inch (7.5-cm) strip grapefruit peel, for garnish

On a small plate, stir together the salt and sugar. Rub the grapefruit wedge alongside half the rim of a rocks glass, then dip the rim in the salt mixture. Set aside.

In a cocktail shaker, combine the grapefruit juice, tequila, and elderflower liqueur, then fill with ice. Cover and shake vigorously until chilled.

Fill the prepared rocks glass with ice, then strain the cocktail into the glass. Add the bitters and top with a splash of sparkling water. Garnish with the grapefruit peel. Enjoy immediately.

With notes of honey and cinnamon—and plenty of citrus—this alcohol-free hot toddy channels the cozy warmth of the original, but with an added dose of heat from infused red chiles to give it a kick. We use dandelion root tea, which has a smooth earthy flavor and detoxifying properties that we especially love during all the festivities of the holiday season. Cheers!

CHILE-SPIKED HOT TODDY

MAKES 4-6 DRINKS

6 cups (48 fl oz/1.4 l) water

5 tablespoons (3¾ oz/110 g) honey, preferably local wildflower honey, or to taste

6 spiced dandelion root tea bags

6 slices lemon, plus more for garnish

6 slices blood orange, plus more for garnish

6 cinnamon sticks, plus more for garnish

4 Thai red chiles or chiles of your choice, wrapped in a cheesecloth bag

Juice of 3 lemons, or to taste

In a medium saucepan over high heat, bring the water to a simmer. Remove the pan from the heat and whisk in the honey until well combined. Add the tea bags, lemon slices, orange slices, cinnamon sticks, and chiles. Let the mixture steep, covered, for 7 minutes.

Stir the lemon juice into the mixture. Taste and adjust for sweetness with more honey or for acidity with more lemon juice if needed. Remove the tea bags and chile bag from the pot and discard. Rewarm over low heat if needed. Ladle into mugs and garnish each with a cinnamon stick, a lemon slice, and an orange slice. Serve immediately.

This is a cross between two hot chocolate schools of thought: cacao ceremonies, which are known to bring happiness, enlightenment, and lots of antioxidants; and rich European-style hot chocolate. This velvety, warm drink emphasizes the superfood powers of cacao while retaining all the delights of a classic hot chocolate and is perfect when you need uplifting.

HAPPY HOT CHOCOLATE

MAKES 4-8 DRINKS

2 cups (16 fl oz/475 ml) unsweetened almond milk, plus more to taste

¾ cup (6 fl oz/180 ml) cashew milk (see Tip), plus more to taste

3 tablespoons maple syrup or date syrup, plus more to taste

¼ teaspoon pure vanilla extract or vanilla bean paste

¼ teaspoon ground cinnamon, preferably Ceylon

1 tablespoon maca root powder (optional)

Pinch of cayenne pepper (optional)

¼ lb (115 g) cacao bar (90–100 percent cacao), chopped, plus more to taste

Pinch of Himalayan pink salt or kosher salt

In a small saucepan, whisk together the almond and cashew milks, maple syrup, vanilla, cinnamon, maca root powder (if using), and cayenne (if using). Bring the mixture to a gentle simmer over medium-low heat. Once the mixture is warm and steaming, remove from the heat, add the cacao and salt, and stir with the whisk until smooth.

Taste and adjust as desired: more syrup for sweetness, more chocolate to thicken, or more milk for a thinner drink. Divide among 4 mugs or 8 small glasses and serve immediately.

TIP *To make cashew milk, soak ¾ cup (3 oz/90 g) raw whole cashews in cold water for 2 hours; for a quicker version, soak the cashews in hot water for 20 minutes, until puffed and softened. Drain through a fine-mesh sieve, discarding the liquid, then add the cashews to a blender along with 1¼ cups (10 fl oz/300 ml) water and a pinch of pink or kosher salt. Blend on high speed until smooth. Strain the mixture through a fine-mesh sieve set over a bowl, pressing on the solids to extract as much liquid as possible. Discard the solids.*

Here in the Test Kitchen, we have an affinity for tequila, so swapping out the vodka for tequila in a classic espresso martini felt like a no-brainer. Make sure to shake the cocktail well and use freshly brewed espresso to create the iconic crema on top of the drink.

TEQUILA ESPRESSO MARTINI

MAKES 1 COCKTAIL

1 fl oz (30 ml) coffee liqueur, such as Kahlúa

1 fl oz (30 ml) freshly brewed medium or dark roast espresso (about 1 shot), chilled

1 fl oz (30 ml) tequila blanco

3 whole coffee beans, for garnish

In a cocktail shaker, combine the coffee liqueur, espresso, and tequila, then add a handful of ice. Cover and shake vigorously until chilled. Strain into a chilled martini glass. Garnish with the coffee beans and serve immediately.

Of course, we had to include a spritz in this book. After all, it's collectively one of the most loved cocktails in the Test Kitchen and the world. Inspired by the classic Aperol Spritz, this citrus cocktail celebrates the connection between the California and Italian coasts—la dolce vita! Clementines would be a nice substitute if you can't find tangerines, but if you can't find either, mandarin oranges will work in a pinch too.

LA DOLCE VITA SPRITZ

MAKES 1 COCKTAIL

1 round slice tangerine

4 fl oz (120 ml) fresh tangerine juice (from about 7 tangerines)

1½ fl oz (45 ml) Campari

4 fl oz (120 ml) prosecco

2–4 fl oz (60–120 ml) club soda

Line a large wineglass with the tangerine wheel. Fill the glass half full with ice. Add the tangerine juice, then the Campari, and then the prosecco. Top with 2 fl oz (60 ml) club soda, adding more if desired. Enjoy immediately.

We love to sip on this antioxidant-rich beverage as a midday pick-me-up or an effervescent alcohol-free option during cocktail hour. You can also try a warm version of this drink in the morning or after dinner to promote healthy digestion. Just omit the ice cubes and sparkling water and use hot water.

GINGER, TURMERIC, AND LEMON TONIC

MAKES 1 DRINK

Juice of ½ lemon, plus 2–3 lemon slices for garnish

1 teaspoon honey, preferably local wildflower honey, or maple syrup

¼ teaspoon packed peeled and grated fresh ginger

¼ teaspoon peeled and grated fresh turmeric, or pinch of ground turmeric

Himalayan pink salt and freshly ground pepper (optional)

¾ cup (6 fl oz/180 ml) sparkling water

In a 12-fl oz (350-ml) tumbler, combine the lemon juice, honey, ginger, and turmeric. Add a small pinch each of salt and pepper if desired, and stir the ingredients to combine. Add a small handful of ice and the lemon slices. Top the mixture with the sparkling water. Stir again to combine, then enjoy.

TIP Although the pinches of salt and pepper are optional, we encourage you to add them to round out both the flavor and health benefits of this drink. The pepper enhances the healing properties of turmeric, and the salt helps promote hydration and balances out the acidic flavors of the drink.

Straight up, we love a margarita. We also love what happens when you combine bright floral flavors like basil with deep, smoky flavors like mezcal. Enter the Fresh Basil Mezcal Margarita, a beautiful, balanced cocktail that will soon become your favorite spring or summer drink. Be sure to peel the lemon before you squeeze the juice to use the whole lemon. And if you love bitters in a cocktail, increase the number of lemon peel strips to three.

FRESH BASIL MEZCAL MARGARITA

MAKES 1 COCKTAIL

11 medium fresh basil leaves,
plus 1 small sprig for garnish (optional)

¾ fl oz (20 ml) fresh lemon juice
(from 1 small lemon)

Two 3-inch (7.5-cm) strips lemon peel

¾–1 fl oz (20–30 ml) simple syrup,
homemade (page 213) or purchased

¾ fl oz (20 ml) orange liqueur,
preferably Grand Marnier

2 fl oz (60 ml) mezcal blanco

Fill a rocks glass three-quarters full with ice. Set aside.

In a cocktail shaker, combine the basil and lemon juice. Muddle together about 20 times (the more you muddle, the greener your cocktail) to release the juices. Add the lemon peels and muddle 5 more times.

Add the simple syrup, orange liqueur, and mezcal to the shaker, then add a handful of ice cubes. Cover and shake vigorously until chilled.

Strain into the prepared rocks glass, garnish with the basil sprig, if using, and enjoy immediately.

A blanco-type tequila is the key to balancing the rich, creamy coconut flavor in this margarita. Unlike reposado and añejo tequilas, blanco isn't aged, so there are no notes of oak from the barrels. Instead you get the essence of sweet, floral agave, an excellent pairing with the lime juice and orange liqueur.

COCONUT CREAM MARGARITA

MAKES 1 COCKTAIL

1 teaspoon kosher salt

1 teaspoon sugar

1 teaspoon finely grated lime zest

2 lime wedges

2 fl oz (60 ml) coconut cream
or cream of coconut

1½ fl oz (45 ml) tequila blanco

1 fl oz (30 ml) fresh lime juice

½ fl oz (15 ml) orange liqueur,
preferably Cointreau

¼ fl oz (7 ml) simple syrup (page 213)

On a small plate, stir together the salt, sugar, and lime zest; spread into an even layer. Gently rub 1 of the lime wedges around the rim of a rocks glass, then dip the rim into the salt mixture. Refrigerate until ready to use.

Fill the rocks glass with ice. In a cocktail shaker, combine the coconut cream, tequila, lime juice, orange liqueur, and simple syrup, then fill with ice. Cover and shake vigorously until chilled.

Strain into the glass. Garnish with the remaining lime wedge and serve immediately.

Since our Coconut Cream Margarita was such a hit, we wanted to create a similar drink without the alcohol but with the same excitement and freshness of a margarita. So we removed the tequila and added flavorful, good-for-you ingredients: citrus juice, honey, ginger, and maca root powder. Enjoy any time of day.

COCONUT CREAM REFRESHER

MAKES 1 DRINK

1 tablespoon fine pink Himalayan salt

Chile-lime seasoning, preferably Tajín Clásico

2 lime wedges

3 fl oz (90 ml) unsweetened coconut milk

2 fl oz (60 ml) each fresh orange juice and
fresh lime juice

1 tablespoon honey, preferably
local wildflower honey

1 teaspoon peeled and grated fresh ginger

¼ teaspoon maca root powder

On a small plate, stir together the salt and ½ teaspoon chile-lime seasoning; spread into an even layer. Gently rub 1 of the lime wedges around the rim of a rocks glass, then dip the rim into the salt mixture. Refrigerate until ready to use.

Fill the rocks glass with ice. In a cocktail shaker, combine the coconut milk, orange juice, lime juice, honey, ginger, maca root powder, and ⅛ teaspoon chile-lime seasoning. Cover and shake vigorously until chilled.

Strain into the glass. Garnish with the remaining lime wedge and a light sprinkle of the chile-lime seasoning. Serve immediately.

BREAKFAST
& BRUNCH

This frittata is dedicated to Devon's mother, Susie Fragnoli, who would make a frittata for nearly any occasion—if it was on the menu, it was a gesture of love. This simple recipe is a great way to use up any seasonal produce in the house and is easy to throw together at the last minute. Whether you are hosting a holiday gathering with family, an impromptu dinner with friends, or a lazy Sunday brunch, this frittata will let everyone at the table know they are welcomed, nourished, and loved.

FARMERS' MARKET FRITTATA

MAKES 6 SERVINGS

3 tablespoons neutral oil, such as avocado

1 leek, white and pale green parts only, diced, or 1 small red or yellow onion, diced

2 cloves garlic, sliced

Kosher salt and freshly ground pepper

2 cups (8 oz/225 g) cut-up seasonal vegetables, such as chopped asparagus, shaved carrots, diced broccoli, diced zucchini, diced mushrooms, or chopped radishes

1 tablespoon chopped fresh seasonal herbs, such as rosemary, thyme, tarragon, basil, or dill

12 large eggs

½ cup (4 fl oz/120 ml) whole milk or plant-based milk

½ cup (2 oz/60 g) grated Parmesan cheese

¼ cup (1 oz/30 g) of another grated cheese such as Cheddar or pecorino, plus more for garnish

FOR GARNISH (OPTIONAL)
Finely grated seasonal citrus zest

Extra-virgin olive oil

Chopped fresh herbs and/or arugula

Basil pesto, homemade (page 212) or purchased

Avocado slices

Preheat the oven to 350°F (180°C).

In a 10-inch (25-cm) ovenproof nonstick or cast-iron frying pan, heat the neutral oil over medium-high heat. Add the leek and garlic and cook, stirring, for 1 minute. Add a large pinch of salt and continue to cook until softened, about 1 minute longer.

Add the vegetables and herbs, then season with salt and pepper. Cook until the vegetables are fork-tender and any extra liquid is released and evaporated, 2–5 minutes. Remove from the heat and set aside.

In a medium bowl, whisk the eggs together until smooth. Whisk in the milk, cheese, 1½ teaspoons salt, and a few grinds of pepper. Whisk in two-thirds of the cooked vegetables. Transfer the remaining vegetables to a separate bowl and set aside.

Carefully pour the egg-vegetable mixture into the frying pan. Transfer to the oven and bake for 10 minutes. Arrange the reserved vegetables on the surface of the frittata. Continue to bake until the frittata is slightly jiggly in the middle and puffs up, about 10 minutes longer; it will set further when cooling. Transfer to a wire rack and let cool for 5–10 minutes.

Serve garnished with citrus zest, a drizzle of olive oil, some grated cheese, along with herbs and/or arugula if desired. A dollop of pesto or a few slices of avocado alongside are also good additions.

Savory quiche makes an impressive centerpiece for a springtime brunch. The leeks are sliced two ways before cooking: two are cut into rounds and one is halved lengthwise. Ready-to-use phyllo dough streamlines prep and gives your creation a fanciful finish.

PHYLLO LEEK AND PARMESAN QUICHE

MAKES 6 SERVINGS

8 sheets phyllo dough, each about 14 by 18 inches (35 by 45 cm), thawed

3 leeks, trimmed, white and light green parts only

4 tablespoons (2 oz/60 g) unsalted butter

2 tablespoons extra-virgin olive oil

1 small yellow onion, diced

Kosher salt and freshly ground pepper

1½ cups (12 fl oz/350 ml) heavy cream

4 large eggs plus 1 large egg yolk

1½ cups (6 oz/170 g) grated Parmesan cheese

Preheat the oven to 375°F (190°C). Lightly grease an 8- or 9-inch (20- or 23-cm) tart pan with 2-inch (5-cm) sides.

On a work surface, lay the 8 phyllo sheets on top of one another, alternating each sheet 90 degrees. Transfer to the prepared tart pan, gently pressing and crimping the phyllo into the bottom and up the sides. Trim the edges, leaving a ½-inch (12-mm) overhang, and crimp the edges slightly. Refrigerate until ready to use.

Slice 2 of the leeks crosswise into ¼-inch (6-mm) rounds, then cut the remaining leek in half lengthwise. In a large frying pan over medium heat, melt 3 tablespoons of the butter with 1 tablespoon of the oil. Add the leek rounds and onion and cook, stirring occasionally, until softened and caramelized, 15–20 minutes. Season with salt and pepper. Transfer to a bowl and let cool.

In the same pan over medium-high heat, melt the remaining 1 tablespoon butter with the remaining 1 tablespoon oil. Add the leek halves, cut side down, and cook until browned and caramelized, about 1 minute. Reduce the heat to medium, cover, and cook until just tender, about 1 minute. Remove from the heat.

In a large bowl, whisk together the cream, whole eggs, and egg yolk. Stir in 1 cup (4 oz/115 g) of the cheese, 1½ teaspoons salt, and ½ teaspoon pepper.

Spoon the leek-onion mixture evenly over the phyllo in the tart pan, then pour in the egg mixture. Arrange the leek halves, cut side up, on top and sprinkle with the remaining ½ cup (2 oz/55 g) cheese.

Bake until the phyllo is golden and the filling is set around the edges but jiggles ever so slightly in the center, about 35 minutes; if the phyllo browns too quickly, cover the quiche with aluminum foil. Let cool on a wire rack for at least 10 minutes before serving.

An ode to the classic Italian dish *uova in purgatorio* (eggs in purgatory), this morning favorite combines spicy tomato sauce with perfectly runny eggs and nutty Parmesan for one of the most comforting breakfasts ever. You'll want to have plenty of crusty bread on hand to mop up every delicious bit.

SPICY BAKED EGGS WITH TOMATOES

MAKES 5 SERVINGS

3 tablespoons olive oil

1 large yellow onion, diced

3 cloves garlic, thinly sliced

1½ cups (9 oz/250 g) cherry tomatoes

2 tablespoons balsamic vinegar

2 teaspoons red pepper flakes, plus more to taste

Kosher salt and freshly ground black pepper

1 can (28 oz/800 g) diced tomatoes with juices

½ cup (2 oz/60 g) grated Parmesan cheese

5 large eggs

1 vine-ripened tomato, thinly sliced

Fresh oregano leaves, for garnish

Crusty bread, for serving

Preheat the oven to 400°F (200°C).

In a large cast-iron frying pan over medium heat, warm the olive oil. Add the onion and cook, stirring occasionally, until softened, about 7 minutes. Add the garlic and cook, stirring occasionally, until fragrant, about 3 minutes.

Add the cherry tomatoes and cook, stirring occasionally and gently crushing them with the back of a wooden spoon, until they have softened and burst, 10–12 minutes. Add the vinegar and red pepper flakes and cook, stirring occasionally, until the vinegar has evaporated, about 1 minute. Season to taste with salt and black pepper.

Add the canned tomatoes and their juices, increase the heat to high, and bring to a vigorous simmer. Cook, stirring occasionally, until the liquid has reduced slightly, about 7 minutes. Stir in half of the Parmesan cheese. Using the back of a spoon, make 5 wells in the tomato sauce and crack an egg into each one. Season the eggs with salt and black pepper. Arrange the tomato slices around the eggs and sprinkle everything with red pepper flakes and the remaining cheese.

Transfer the pan to the oven and bake until the egg whites are set and the yolks are still runny, 10–13 minutes, or until done to your liking. Garnish with the oregano and serve immediately with crusty bread alongside.

Although many people know this dish as toad in the hole or egg in a hole, Belle grew up calling it bunnies in a hole (the origin unknown but the name extremely cute!). This nostalgic breakfast—toasty buttered bread, bacon, and a runny egg—never gets old.

BUNNIES IN A HOLE

MAKES 4 SERVINGS

8 slices thick-cut bacon

4 slices country-style bread, each ½ inch (12 mm) thick

4 tablespoons (2 oz/60 g) unsalted butter, at room temperature

Kosher salt and freshly ground pepper

½ cup (2 oz/60 g) grated Parmesan cheese

4 large eggs

3 tablespoons chopped fresh flat-leaf parsley leaves, or 8 fresh chives, snipped

Preheat the oven to 400°F (200°C). Place the bacon slices in a single layer on a baking sheet. Bake until the fat begins to render and the bacon is lightly browned but not yet crisp, about 7 minutes. Transfer the bacon to a paper towel–lined plate.

Using paper towels, wipe off the excess fat from the baking sheet, leaving a thin layer behind. Using a 3-inch (7.5-cm) round biscuit cutter or the rim of a similar-size glass, cut a hole in the center of each bread slice. Spread the bread slices and cutouts on both sides with the butter. Season lightly with salt and pepper and sprinkle with the Parmesan. Place the bread slices and cutouts on the baking sheet, spacing them at least 1 inch (2.5 cm) apart. Crisscross 2 bacon slices over the hole in each bread slice, pressing the bacon gently into the hole to create a "nest" for the egg.

Bake until the bread is lightly toasted and the cheese is melted, about 5 minutes. Remove from the oven and carefully crack an egg into each bacon "nest." Season the eggs with salt and pepper. Continue baking until the whites are set but the yolks are still runny, 5–7 minutes. Divide among 4 plates, sprinkle with the parsley, and serve immediately.

TIP *If you don't have Parmesan on hand, you can use whatever cheese is in your fridge—Gruyère would be delish. Tarragon would make another good substitute for the parsley, or you can skip the herb entirely.*

We love this hearty recipe for when you have company but want a casual meal. Once you make the tomatillo sauce—which can be stored in the fridge for a week—it couldn't be easier to throw together. Crema, which is the more classic accompaniment, can be used in place of the Greek yogurt.

SKILLET CHILAQUILES VERDE

MAKES 4 SERVINGS

FOR THE TOMATILLO SAUCE
2 lb (1 kg) tomatillos, husks and stems removed

1–2 serrano chiles, depending on desired heat (optional)

1 poblano chile

4 cloves garlic

1 white onion, quartered

¼ cup (½ oz/15 g) packed cilantro leaves and stems

1 cup (8 fl oz/240 ml) vegetable stock, homemade (page 203) or purchased

Kosher salt

1 tablespoon neutral oil, such as avocado

1 bag (12 oz/340 g) thick-cut corn tortilla chips

4 large eggs, fried or scrambled (optional)

Kosher salt and freshly ground pepper

½ cup (4 oz/115 g) plain Greek yogurt thinned with ¼ cup (2 fl oz/60 ml) water

¼ cup (1¼ oz/35 g) crumbled Cotija cheese

1 green onion, thinly sliced

½ cup (1 oz/30 g) loosely packed fresh cilantro leaves, roughly chopped

½ cup (1 oz/30 g) arugula, finely chopped (optional)

Sliced avocado, for serving

To make the tomatillo sauce, line a baking sheet with parchment paper. Preheat the oven to broil. Rinse the sticky residue from the tomatillos, then dry and quarter them. Stem, halve lengthwise, and seed the serrano (if using) and poblano chiles. Arrange the tomatillos, chiles, and garlic on the pan, spacing them out evenly. Broil the vegetables until blistered and tender, about 12 minutes. Remove and set aside to cool for 10 minutes.

In a blender, combine the broiled vegetables, onion, cilantro, vegetable stock, and 1 teaspoon salt and blend on medium speed until combined and smooth, about 1 minute.

In a frying pan over medium-high heat, warm the oil. Add the tomatillo sauce and cook, stirring, until slightly thickened, about 5 minutes. Taste and season with more salt if needed. If desired, let the sauce cool, then transfer to an airtight container and refrigerate for up to 1 week. Reheat before using.

In three batches, add the chips to the warm tomatillo sauce, stirring and tossing to coat the chips and breaking up some of the chips as you toss.

Divide the chilaquiles among 4 plates, including 1 egg for each portion, if using. Drizzle with the yogurt and sprinkle with the cheese, green onion, cilantro, and arugula (if using). Top with the avocado slices and serve.

TIP *We prefer Greek yogurt here for its tartness and because it's a healthier option.*

This is a brunch favorite that never goes out of style. Here, we swap in earthy chard for the spinach and fry the eggs instead of poaching them. For savory-salty goodness, we also added crisp slices of thick-cut bacon. Chopped fresh tarragon lends a mild anise flavor to the rich hollandaise.

EGGS FLORENTINE WITH TARRAGON HOLLANDAISE

MAKES 2 SERVINGS

FOR THE TARRAGON HOLLANDAISE

1 cup (8 oz/225 g) unsalted butter

1 large egg plus 2 large egg yolks

1 tablespoon fresh lemon juice

⅛ teaspoon cayenne pepper

2 tablespoons finely chopped fresh tarragon

1 tablespoon water

Kosher salt and freshly ground black pepper

4 slices thick-cut bacon (about ¼ lb/115 g)

½ lb (225 g) Swiss or rainbow chard, stems removed and leaves coarsely chopped

Juice of ½ lemon

Kosher salt and freshly ground black pepper

2 tablespoons unsalted butter

2 English muffins, split

4 large eggs

Pinch of cayenne pepper

Flake salt

Coarsely cut fresh chives or microgreens, for garnish

To make the hollandaise, in a saucepan over low heat, melt the butter; keep warm. In a food processor, combine the whole egg and egg yolks, lemon juice, and cayenne and process until smooth. With the processor running, slowly add the butter and process until incorporated, about 1 minute. Transfer the sauce to the saucepan, set over low heat, and cook, whisking constantly, until it is slightly thickened and coats the back of a spoon, about 1 minute. Remove from the heat, whisk in the tarragon and water, season with kosher salt and black pepper, and keep warm.

In a large nonstick frying pan over medium-high heat, cook the bacon, turning once and reducing the heat to medium halfway through, until browned and crisp, about 3 minutes per side. Transfer to a paper towel–lined plate. Pour off all but 1 tablespoon of the fat, return the pan to medium heat, add the chard and lemon juice, and season with kosher salt and black pepper. Cook, tossing, until just wilted, 1–2 minutes. Transfer to a bowl. Wipe out the pan.

In the frying pan over medium heat, melt 1 tablespoon of the butter. Add the English muffin halves, cut side down, and cook until toasted and golden brown, about 1 minute. Place 2 muffin halves, cut side up, on each of 2 individual plates.

In the frying pan over medium heat, melt the remaining 1 tablespoon butter. Crack the eggs into the pan, reduce the heat to medium-low, cover, and fry until the whites are set but the yolks are runny, about 2 minutes. Season with kosher salt and black pepper and the cayenne.

To assemble, divide the chard among the English muffin halves. Top with a piece of bacon and a fried egg. Spoon the hollandaise over the top of each serving. Sprinkle with flake salt, garnish with chives, and serve immediately.

Our dairy-free oatmeal, which uses coconut milk instead of regular milk, is a great way to feed a small group of friends or family at brunch or breakfast. The coconut milk makes this dish super comforting and rich, while the berry compote adds a nice freshness and tang. We call for blueberries and raspberries, but use whatever berries you love. The compote can be prepared up to a week in advance to give you a jump-start on those sleepy mornings.

COCONUT OATMEAL WITH BERRY COMPOTE

MAKES 4–6 SERVINGS

FOR THE BERRY COMPOTE
2 cups (10 oz/285 g) fresh blueberries

1½ cups (6 oz/170 g) fresh raspberries

Finely grated zest and juice of 1 lemon

1 tablespoon maple syrup

1 teaspoon chia seeds

¼ teaspoon rosewater (optional)

⅛ teaspoon ground cinnamon

Kosher salt

1½ teaspoons arrowroot powder
or cornstarch

FOR THE OATMEAL
2 cans (each 13½ fl oz/400 ml)
unsweetened coconut milk, ¼ cup
(2 fl oz/60 ml) reserved for serving

2¼ cups (18 fl oz/535 ml) water

2 cups (7 oz/200 g) gluten-free
rolled oats

3 tablespoons maple syrup,
or to taste

⅛ teaspoon ground cinnamon

Kosher salt

1 vanilla bean, split lengthwise,
or 1 tablespoon vanilla bean paste
or pure vanilla extract

Toasted coconut flakes, for garnish

To make the berry compote, in a medium saucepan over medium heat, combine the blueberries, raspberries, lemon zest and juice, maple syrup, chia seeds, rosewater (if using), cinnamon, and a pinch of salt. Cook, stirring gently, until the mixture is lightly bubbling and juicy and the berries darken in color, about 5 minutes. Remove from the heat and gently fold in the arrowroot. Set aside to use right away, or let cool and store in an airtight container in the refrigerator for up to 1 week.

To make the oatmeal, in a large saucepan over medium-high heat, combine the coconut milk and water, bring to a boil, then reduce the heat to medium-low. Stir in the oats, maple syrup, cinnamon, and 2 pinches of salt. Scrape the vanilla bean seeds into the pan and add the pod, or add the vanilla bean paste or extract. Stir to combine. Cook, stirring occasionally, until the oats are tender and have doubled in volume, about 14 minutes for looser oatmeal and about 17 minutes for thicker oatmeal. Remove from the heat and remove and discard the vanilla bean pod, if using.

Ladle the oatmeal into bowls and top with the berry compote. Garnish with the coconut flakes and a drizzle of coconut milk and serve immediately.

These savory popovers are transformed into a full meal with the addition of poached eggs and a tangle of watercress. For a perfect poach, use the freshest eggs and be sure to drain the whites through a fine-mesh sieve so the eggs hold their shape while cooking.

PARMESAN-PARSLEY POPOVERS WITH POACHED EGGS AND GREENS

MAKES 6 SERVINGS

FOR THE PARMESAN-PARSLEY POPOVERS

4 large eggs, at room temperature

1½ cups (12 fl oz/350 ml) whole milk, heated to 120°F (49°C)

1½ cups (6½ oz/185 g) all-purpose flour

2 tablespoons sugar

1 teaspoon kosher salt

3 tablespoons unsalted butter, melted and cooled slightly

¼ cup (½ oz/15 g) minced fresh flat-leaf parsley leaves

½ cup (2 oz/60 g) freshly grated Parmesan cheese, plus more for topping

FOR THE TOPPINGS

6 large eggs

2 bunches watercress, leaves and tender stems, or 3 cups baby arugula

Extra-virgin olive oil

Squeeze of fresh lemon juice

Kosher salt and freshly ground black pepper

Salted butter, at room temperature, for serving

Red pepper flakes, for garnish

To make the popovers, in a blender, process the eggs, milk, flour, sugar, and salt on high speed until smooth, about 30 seconds. Add the melted butter and blend until combined, about 10 seconds. Add the parsley and Parmesan and pulse once or twice to mix. Let rest for 15 minutes.

Position a rack in the lower third of the oven and preheat to 450°F (230°C). Place a 6-cup popover pan on a baking sheet and place in the preheated oven for 5 minutes. Stir the batter briefly to evenly disperse the ingredients, then spray each cup with cooking spray and divide the batter evenly among the cups; they should be three-quarters full.

Bake the popovers without opening the oven door for 20 minutes. Reduce the oven temperature to 350°F (180°C) and continue to bake until they are deeply browned and sound hollow when lightly tapped, about 10 minutes longer.

Meanwhile, prepare the toppings. First, poach the eggs as directed in the recipe on page 51, or according to your favorite method. Then, just before serving, in a bowl, toss the watercress with a drizzle of oil and the lemon juice and season with salt and black pepper.

Carefully transfer the popovers to a wire rack. Using a paring knife, cut a small slit in the side of each popover to release some of the steam and let sit for a couple of minutes. Then divide among individual plates, slice open, and spread with the room-temperature butter. Top each popover with a poached egg and sprinkle with salt and red pepper flakes. Serve warm with the dressed watercress alongside.

Cake for breakfast? Well, while we were developing (and devouring) this recipe, we constantly craved a latte or cup of dark-roast coffee to wash it down. So, we deemed it a treat to enjoy on a leisurely Sunday morning. The flavors are rich and pronounced, while the texture is tender thanks to the sour cream and Dutch-process cocoa powder.

CHOCOLATE ESPRESSO MARBLE CAKE

MAKES 10–12 SERVINGS

1½ cups (12 oz/340 g) unsalted butter, at room temperature

1½ cups (10½ oz/300 g) sugar

4 large eggs plus 2 large egg yolks, at room temperature

½ cup (4 oz/115 g) sour cream

2 tablespoons vanilla bean paste or pure vanilla extract

2½ teaspoons kosher salt

1½ cups (6½ oz/180 g) cake flour

⅓ cup (1 oz/30 g) plus 1 tablespoon Dutch-process cocoa powder

2 teaspoons espresso powder mixed with 2 teaspoons hot water

Preheat the oven to 350°F (180°C). Grease and flour a 10- to 12-cup (2.5- to 3-l) Bundt pan or a 1½-lb (680-g) loaf pan. Place the pan on a rimmed baking sheet.

In the bowl of a stand mixer fitted with the paddle attachment, beat together the butter and sugar on medium speed until light and fluffy, about 5 minutes. Add the wholes eggs and egg yolks one at a time and beat until fully incorporated, about 1 minute. Stop the mixer and scrape down the sides of the bowl. Add the sour cream, vanilla, and salt and beat on medium speed until combined, about 1 minute.

Divide the batter equally between 2 bowls. Sift 1 cup (4¼ oz/120 g) of the flour into the batter in one bowl, then fold in the flour with a rubber spatula until no dry streaks remain. This is the vanilla batter. Sift the remaining ½ cup (2 oz/60 g) flour and the cocoa powder into the second bowl and fold into the batter until no dry streaks remain, then stir in the espresso mixture. This is the chocolate batter.

Pour about one-third of the vanilla batter into the prepared pan, then top with about one-third of the chocolate batter. Continue adding the vanilla and chocolate batters in alternating layers to make a total of six layers. In one continuous "S" formation, drag a table knife through the batter to create a swirl, then switch directions and swirl again. Repeat the swirling in both directions two more times until the batter is nicely swirled.

Bake until a toothpick inserted into the center of the cake comes out clean, about 55 minutes if using a Bundt pan and 1 hour 25 minutes if using a loaf pan. Transfer the pan to a wire rack and let cool for 15 minutes, then invert the pan onto the rack and lift off the pan. Serve warm or at room temperature.

Rich, egg-based breads like challah and brioche make the best French toast since they soak up the custard well, especially if left overnight. So assemble this dish the night before serving for an easy, breezy morning. We love adding vanilla seeds straight from the bean because they give the toast a beautiful speckled look and strong flavor, but feel free to substitute 2–3 teaspoons vanilla bean paste or 1 tablespoon pure vanilla extract.

MAKE-AHEAD VANILLA BEAN FRENCH TOAST

MAKES 4 SERVINGS

1 loaf challah or brioche
(about 1 lb/450 g), cut into slices
1 inch (2.5 cm) thick

6 large eggs, lightly beaten

2 cups (16 fl oz/475 ml) half-and-half

¼ cup (2 oz/60 g) firmly packed
light brown sugar

1 teaspoon finely grated lemon zest

Pinch of kosher salt

1 vanilla bean, split lengthwise

½ cup (5½ oz/155 g) maple syrup

2 tablespoons unsalted butter

1 teaspoon pure vanilla extract

½ cup (2 oz/60 g) fresh raspberries

¼ cup (1 oz/30 g) sliced almonds

Confectioners' sugar, for dusting

TIP **If you opt to skip the vanilla bean garnish, you can reserve the bean for another use. We like making vanilla-flavored sugar—just place the scraped vanilla bean in a sealable glass jar, cover with granulated sugar, and let sit overnight to allow the flavors to infuse. Use the sugar as directed in your favorite dessert recipe.**

Preheat the oven to 425°F (220°C). Butter the bottom and sides of a 9-by-13-inch (23-by-33-cm) baking dish. Set aside.

Arrange the bread slices in a single layer on a baking sheet. Toast until the bread is lightly golden brown and dry, about 7 minutes, turning once halfway through. Transfer to a wire rack and let cool.

In a large bowl, whisk together the eggs, half-and-half, brown sugar, lemon zest, and salt. Using a paring knife, scrape the seeds from the vanilla bean halves into the egg mixture and whisk to combine; reserve the vanilla bean halves. Working in batches, dip the bread slices into the egg mixture, turning the slices to coat them and letting the bread sit in the bowl for about 2 minutes to absorb the liquid.

Arrange the bread slices in the prepared baking dish, overlapping them. Pour any remaining egg mixture over the bread. Cover with aluminum foil and refrigerate for at least 2 hours or up to overnight.

Preheat the oven to 350°F (180°C). Transfer the dish, still covered with the foil, to the oven and bake for 30 minutes. Uncover the dish, increase the oven temperature to 375°F (190°C), and continue baking until the French toast is puffed up and browned, about 15 minutes more.

While the French toast is baking, in a small saucepan over low heat, combine the maple syrup and butter. Cook, stirring occasionally, until the butter has melted, about 4 minutes. Remove from the heat and stir in the vanilla extract.

Pour the maple syrup mixture evenly over the French toast, then sprinkle with the berries and almonds and garnish with the reserved vanilla bean halves if desired. Dust with confectioners' sugar and serve.

When Belle was growing up, her mom made a version of these cinnamon-sugary drop donuts every Christmas morning. And while that tradition inspired this recipe, these donuts are the perfect way to sweeten up any morning. Enjoy with a cup of coffee or tea. If you cannot find sugar plum jam, raspberry and blackberry jam are equally delicious.

CHRISTMAS MORNING DROP DONUTS WITH SUGAR PLUM JAM

MAKES ABOUT 30 DONUTS

2 cups (9 oz/240 g) all-purpose flour

½ cup (3½ oz/100 g) plus
1 cup (7 oz/200 g) sugar

1¼ teaspoons baking powder

½ teaspoon baking soda

¾ teaspoon kosher salt

1 cup (8 fl oz/240 ml) buttermilk

1 large egg

4 tablespoons (2 oz/60 g) unsalted butter, melted and cooled slightly

2 teaspoons pure vanilla extract

1 tablespoon ground cinnamon

Oil for frying, such as canola

Sugar plum jam, for serving

In a large bowl, whisk together the flour, ½ cup (3½ oz/100 g) sugar, baking powder, baking soda, and salt. In a large measuring cup, whisk together the buttermilk and egg. Pour into the dry ingredients, then add the melted butter and vanilla. Mix just until thoroughly combined; do not overmix. Let rest at room temperature for 30–60 minutes.

Meanwhile, in a wide bowl, stir together the remaining 1 cup (7 oz/200 g) sugar and the cinnamon. Set aside.

Pour about 1½ inches (4 cm) of oil into a heavy-bottomed saucepan. Heat to 375°F (190°C) on a deep-frying thermometer. Line a plate with paper towels and set next to the stove.

Spray a 1½-inch (4-cm) cookie scoop with cooking spray. Working in batches to avoid overcrowding, scoop up the batter and gently drop it into the oil. Cook, turning once with tongs, until deep golden brown, 1½–2 minutes. Transfer to the prepared plate to drain.

Continue to fry the donuts, making sure not to overcrowd the pan. If the scoop gets too sticky with batter, wipe it down and spray again with cooking spray.

While the donuts are still warm, toss them in the cinnamon sugar until evenly coated. Serve warm with the sugar plum jam.

This quick and satisfying all-in-one meal is ideal for a relaxed weekend brunch when you want to serve something delicious but not do a ton of dishes the rest of the morning (in other words: more time for mimosas!). We love this with plenty of chili crisp and some crunchy country-style bread.

SHEET PAN BREAKY POTATOES WITH BANGERS AND EGGS

MAKES 4 SERVINGS

3–4 large Yukon Gold potatoes (about 1¼ lb total weight), cut into ½-inch (12-mm) cubes and patted dry

3 tablespoons olive oil

2 teaspoons granulated garlic

2 teaspoons granulated onion

2 teaspoons smoked or sweet paprika

Kosher salt and freshly ground pepper

4 sausages, such as bangers, bratwursts, sweet Italian sausages, or large breakfast sausages (about 13 oz/370 g total weight)

4–8 large eggs

Lena's Chili Crisp (page 210), for serving

Preheat the oven to 425°F (220°C). Place the potatoes in a large bowl and toss with the oil, granulated garlic, granulated onion, paprika, 1½ teaspoons salt, and a few generous grinds of pepper.

Transfer to a nonstick rimmed baking sheet and spread into an even layer. Roast for 20 minutes, then turn the potatoes. Add the sausages to the baking sheet, moving the potatoes as needed to make room for them. Continue to cook until the potatoes are crisp and browned and the sausages are browned and heated through, 15–17 minutes longer.

Remove the baking sheet from the oven, toss the potatoes and turn the sausages, then create 4–8 spaces for the eggs in among the sausages and potatoes. Crack an egg into each space. Season the eggs with salt and pepper.

Bake until the egg whites are set but the yolks are still runny, about 4 minutes. Serve immediately, topped with the chili crisp.

A mash-up of two of our favorites—tater tots and waffles—this is sure to be in regular rotation when you want a comforting brunch. These crispy tot waffles are loaded with three kinds of cheese: sharp Cheddar, Gruyère, and Parmesan. We love adding a dollop of crème fraîche and chives, but you can really go to town with sliced avocado, poached eggs (page 51), and Lena's Chili Crisp (page 210) on top. So have fun!

CHEESY POTATO WAFFLES

MAKES 4 WAFFLES

2 lb (1 kg) frozen tater tots, thawed (about 8 cups)

1 cup (4 oz/115 g) shredded sharp white Cheddar cheese

½ cup (2 oz/60 g) shredded aged Gruyère cheese

½ cup (2 oz/60 g) shredded Parmesan cheese

½ teaspoon onion powder (optional)

1 teaspoon kosher salt

Freshly ground pepper

½ cup (4 oz/115 g) crème fraîche, sour cream, or plain yogurt

1 tablespoon chopped fresh chives

Preheat a Belgian waffle iron to medium-high (typically heat setting 4). Place a baking sheet in the oven and preheat to 200°F (95°C).

In a medium bowl, combine the tater tots, Cheddar, Gruyère, Parmesan, onion powder (if using), salt, and a couple of grindings of pepper. Set aside.

Lightly grease the waffle iron with cooking spray. Evenly spread with about 1½ cups (6 oz/170 g) of the tater tot mixture per waffle. Close the waffle iron and cook for 2 minutes.

Open the waffle iron and fill in any holes in the waffle with the tater tot mixture (about ½ cup/3 oz/90 g per waffle), breaking the tater tots into pieces if needed. Close the waffle iron and continue to cook until golden and crispy, about 4 minutes longer. Using a metal spatula, carefully remove the waffles and transfer to the baking sheet in the oven to keep warm. Repeat to cook the remaining waffles.

To serve, top each warm waffle with 2 tablespoons crème fraîche then garnish with chives and more pepper. Serve immediately.

We tested this recipe for scones more times than we can count to achieve the perfect flaky, soft interior while keeping the iconic triangular structure. The result is a batch of buttery beauties that are quick—though a little messy—to throw together, just as scones should be, and are so good that we have converted scone haters into scone lovers with this recipe alone. The dough can even be made 3 days ahead and kept chilled before cutting, brushing, and baking for a make-ahead moment.

OUR GO-TO BUTTERMILK SCONES

MAKES 8 SCONES

2 large eggs

½ cup (4 fl oz/120 ml) plus
1 tablespoon cold buttermilk

3 cups (12¾ oz/360 g) all-purpose flour

⅓ cup (2½ oz/70 g) plus
2 tablespoons granulated sugar,
plus more for sprinkling

1½ teaspoons baking powder

¾ teaspoon kosher salt

1 cup (8 oz/225 g) cold unsalted butter,
cut into ½-inch (12-mm) pieces

Turbinado sugar, for garnish

In a large bowl, lightly whisk the eggs until blended, then whisk in ½ cup (4 fl oz/120 ml) of the buttermilk. Set aside.

In a food processor, combine the flour, granulated sugar, baking powder, and salt and pulse until blended. Add the butter and pulse until moist, pea-size crumbs form; be careful not to overprocess.

Add the flour mixture to the egg mixture. Using your hands or a rubber spatula, quickly combine just until the dough comes together and looks shaggy.

Turn the dough out onto a lightly floured work surface and gather into a ball. If the dough is too crumbly to shape and cut, knead once or twice before shaping into a ball. Gently press down with your palm to flatten, then shape the dough into an 8-inch (20-cm) round. Wrap in plastic wrap and freeze for 30 minutes or refrigerate up to overnight.

Preheat the oven to 425°F (220°C). Line a baking sheet with parchment paper.

Using a bench scraper or a knife, cut the dough disk into 8 equal wedges. Transfer to the prepared baking sheet, spacing the scones evenly apart. Brush the tops of the scones with the remaining 1 tablespoon buttermilk and sprinkle generously with turbinado sugar.

Bake until the scones are lightly golden and a toothpick inserted into the center comes out clean, about 20 minutes. Transfer the scones to a wire rack and let cool for at least 5 minutes before serving.

This scone is for the *cacio e pepe* (Italian for "cheese and pepper") lovers! "I tend to serve my guests this savory scone in a fun breakfast spread after a morning hike up some of the classic San Francisco hills. I also leave extras in a glass jar for snacks and a homey feel," says Devon. They're fabulous plain, but we recommend serving this scone with a side of crème fraîche and crispy prosciutto or alongside our bistro-inspired brunch salad on page 51.

CACIO E PEPE SCONES

MAKES 8 SCONES

2 large eggs

½ cup (4 fl oz/120 ml) plus 1 tablespoon cold buttermilk

3 cups (12¾ oz/360 g) all-purpose flour

1½ cups (6 oz/170 g) packed grated Parmesan cheese, plus more for garnish

¾ cup (3 oz/90 g) packed grated pecorino or Gruyère cheese, plus more for garnish

1 tablespoon sugar

1½ teaspoons baking powder

1½ teaspoons freshly ground pepper, plus more for garnish

1¼ teaspoons kosher salt

Pinch of freshly grated nutmeg

1 cup (8 oz/225 g) cold unsalted butter, cut into ½-inch (12-mm) pieces

In a large bowl, lightly whisk the eggs until blended, then whisk in ½ cup (4 fl oz/120 ml) of the buttermilk. Set aside.

In a food processor, combine the flour, cheeses, sugar, baking powder, pepper, salt, and nutmeg and pulse until blended. Add the butter and pulse until moist, pea-size crumbs form; be careful not to overprocess.

Add the flour mixture to the egg mixture. Using your hands or a rubber spatula, quickly combine just until the dough comes together and looks shaggy.

Turn the dough out onto a lightly floured work surface and gather into a ball. If the dough is too crumbly to shape and cut, knead once or twice before shaping into a ball. Gently press down with your palm to flatten, then shape the dough into an 8-inch (20-cm) round. Wrap in plastic wrap and freeze for 15 minutes or refrigerate up to overnight.

Preheat the oven to 425°F (220°C). Line a baking sheet with parchment paper.

Using a bench scraper or a knife, cut the dough disk into 8 equal wedges. Transfer to the prepared baking sheet, spacing the scones evenly apart. Brush the tops of the scones with the remaining 1 tablespoon buttermilk and sprinkle with more pepper, Parmesan, and pecorino.

Bake until the scones are lightly golden and a toothpick inserted into the center comes out clean, about 20 minutes. Transfer the scones to a wire rack and let cool for at least 5 minutes before serving.

This variation on our classic buttermilk scones adds juicy blueberries and tangy lemon zest, resulting in one of our favorite sweet scones. Don't skip out on coating the blueberries in flour—the flour absorbs some of the fruit juices as the scones bake, making the berries less likely to sink to the bottom. We love to eat them straight off the baking sheet, but for a slightly more sophisticated serving suggestion, eat warm with lemon curd and a cup of tea.

SWEET LEMON BLUEBERRY SCONES

MAKES 8 SCONES

2 large eggs

½ cup (4 fl oz/120 ml) plus
1 tablespoon cold buttermilk

1 teaspoon vanilla bean paste
or pure vanilla extract

1 cup (5 oz/140 g) fresh blueberries

3 cups (12¾ oz/360 g) plus
1 tablespoon all-purpose flour

⅓ cup (2½ oz/70 g) plus ¼ cup
(1¾ oz/50 g) granulated sugar

1½ teaspoons baking powder

½ teaspoon kosher salt

Finely grated zest of 1 large lemon

1 cup (8 oz/225 g) cold unsalted butter,
cut into ½-inch (12-mm) pieces

Turbinado sugar, for garnish

In a large bowl, lightly whisk the eggs until blended, then whisk in ½ cup (4 fl oz/120 ml) of the buttermilk and the vanilla bean paste. Set aside.

In a small bowl, toss the blueberries with the 1 tablespoon flour until the blueberries are coated. Set aside.

In a food processor, combine the remaining 3 cups (12¾ oz/360 g) flour with the granulated sugar, baking powder, salt, and lemon zest and pulse until blended. Add the butter and pulse until pea-size crumbs form.

Add the flour mixture to the egg mixture, then add the blueberries. Using your hands or a rubber spatula, quickly combine just until the dough comes together and looks shaggy.

Turn the dough out onto a lightly floured work surface and gather into a ball. If the dough is too crumbly to shape and cut, knead once or twice before shaping into a ball. Gently press down with your palm to flatten, then shape the dough into an 8-inch (20-cm) round. Wrap in plastic wrap and freeze for 15 minutes or refrigerate up to overnight.

Preheat the oven to 425°F (220°C). Line a baking sheet with parchment paper.

Using a bench scraper or a knife, cut the dough disk into 8 equal wedges. Transfer to the prepared baking sheet, spacing the scones evenly apart. Brush the tops of the scones with the remaining 1 tablespoon buttermilk and sprinkle with turbinado sugar.

Bake until the scones are lightly golden and a toothpick inserted into the center comes out clean, about 20 minutes. Transfer the scones to a wire rack and let cool for at least 5 minutes before serving.

A little salty, a little sweet, and *a lot* delicious, this variation on our go-to scone is simply perfect. Seriously, we cannot stop making them...and eating them. The bittersweet chocolate adds depth without being too cloying, but feel free to use whatever chocolate you love. Eat them as is or add a drizzle of melted peanut butter after baking for a decadent treat. Either way, look at this as an excuse to eat a chocolate chip "cookie" for breakfast.

SALTED CHOCOLATE CHIP SCONES

MAKES 8 SCONES

2 large eggs

½ cup (4 fl oz/120 ml) plus
1 tablespoon cold buttermilk

1 teaspoon vanilla bean
paste or pure vanilla extract

3 cups (12¾ oz/360 g) all-purpose flour

⅓ cup (2½ oz/70 g) plus ¼ cup
(1¾ oz/50 g) granulated sugar

1½ teaspoons baking powder

½ teaspoon ground cinnamon,
preferably Ceylon

½ teaspoon fine sea salt

1 cup (8 oz/225 g) cold unsalted butter,
cut into ½-inch (12-mm) pieces

1 cup (6 oz/170 g) semisweet
chocolate disks or chips

Turbinado sugar, for garnish

Flake salt, for garnish

In a large bowl, lightly whisk the eggs until blended, then whisk in ½ cup (4 fl oz/120 ml) of the buttermilk and the vanilla bean paste. Set aside.

In a food processor, combine the flour, granulated sugar, baking powder, cinnamon, and fine salt and pulse until blended. Add the butter and pulse until moist, pea-size crumbs form; be careful not to overprocess.

Add the flour mixture to the egg mixture, then add the chocolate disks. Using your hands or a rubber spatula, quickly combine just until the dough comes together and looks shaggy.

Turn the dough out onto a lightly floured work surface and gather into a ball. If the dough is too crumbly to shape and cut, knead once or twice before shaping into a ball. Gently press down with your palm to flatten, then shape the dough into an 8-inch (20-cm) round. Wrap in plastic wrap and freeze for 15 minutes or refrigerate up to overnight.

Preheat the oven to 425°F (220°C). Line a baking sheet with parchment paper.

Using a bench scraper or a knife, cut the dough disk into 8 equal wedges. Transfer to the prepared baking sheet, spacing the scones evenly apart. Brush the tops of the scones with the remaining 1 tablespoon buttermilk and sprinkle generously with turbinado sugar and flake salt.

Bake until the scones are lightly golden and a toothpick inserted into the center comes out clean, about 20 minutes. Transfer the scones to a wire rack and let cool for at least 5 minutes before serving.

We just love the drama a popover brings to any table. They are wildly tender on the inside with a deeply developed crust, perfect to pair with softened butter and sweet jam. The room-temperature eggs and warm milk are essential for successful popovers, as the emulsion of the ingredients makes them super lofty. Serve these popovers right away they are best warm from the oven.

CLASSIC POPOVERS WITH SALTED BUTTER AND RASPBERRY JAM

MAKES 6 POPOVERS

4 large eggs, at room temperature

1½ cups (12 fl oz/350 ml) whole milk, heated to 120°F (49°C)

1½ cups (6½ oz/180 g) all-purpose flour

2 tablespoons granulated sugar

1 teaspoon kosher salt

3 tablespoons unsalted butter, melted and slightly cooled

Confectioners' sugar, for dusting (optional)

Salted butter, for serving

Raspberry jam, for serving

In a blender, combine the eggs, milk, flour, granulated sugar, and salt. Blend on high speed until smooth, about 30 seconds. Scrape down the sides of the blender and add the melted butter. Blend on high until combined, about 10 seconds. Set aside for 15 minutes for the batter to rest.

Position a rack in the lower third of the oven and preheat to 450°F (230°C). Place a 6-cup popover pan on a rimmed baking sheet. Once the oven is preheated, place the baking sheet and pan into the oven to preheat for 10 minutes.

Carefully spray each cup with cooking spray. Divide the batter evenly among the prepared cups; they should be three-quarters full.

Bake the popovers without opening the oven door for 20 minutes; they will puff up and begin to look browned.

Reduce the oven temperature to 350°F (180°C) and continue to bake until the popovers are deeply browned and sound hollow when lightly tapped, about 10 minutes longer.

Carefully remove the popovers from the pan and transfer to a cooling rack. Using a paring knife, cut a small slit in the side of each popover to release some of the steam.

Dust with confectioners' sugar if desired. Serve warm with salted butter and jam.

No offense to bagels, but we may have just reinvented the wheel. These elegant popovers make for a delicious spread at brunch. We like slicing open the popovers and spreading each with crème fraîche, then layering on salmon and toppings, but you can also serve these family-style, allowing guests to choose their toppings.

POPPY SEED POPOVERS WITH SMOKED SALMON AND CRÈME FRAÎCHE

MAKES 6 SERVINGS

FOR THE POPPY SEED POPOVERS
4 large eggs, at room temperature

1½ cups (12 fl oz/350 ml) whole milk, heated to 120°F (49°C)

1½ cups (6½ oz/180 g) all-purpose flour

2 tablespoons sugar

1 teaspoon kosher salt

3 tablespoons unsalted butter, melted and slightly cooled

1 tablespoon poppy seeds

FOR THE TOPPINGS
1 cup (8 oz/225 g) crème fraîche

½ lb (225 g) smoked salmon

3 tablespoons capers

½ red onion, very thinly sliced

3 tablespoons chopped fresh dill

3 tablespoons minced fresh chives

To make the popovers, in a blender, combine the eggs, milk, flour, sugar, and salt. Blend on high speed until smooth, about 30 seconds. Scrape down the sides of the blender and add the melted butter. Blend on high until combined, about 10 seconds. Add the poppy seeds and pulse once or twice to combine. Set aside for 15 minutes for the batter to rest.

Position a rack in the lower third of the oven and preheat to 450°F (230°C). Place a 6-cup popover pan on a rimmed baking sheet. Once the oven is preheated, place the baking sheet and pan into the oven to preheat for 10 minutes. Stir the batter again to ensure the poppy seeds are dispersed throughout the mixture.

Carefully spray each cup with cooking spray. Divide the batter evenly among the prepared cups; they should be three-quarters full.

Bake the popovers without opening the oven door for 20 minutes; they will puff up and begin to look browned.

Reduce the oven temperature to 350°F (180°C) and continue to bake until the popovers are deeply browned and sound hollow when lightly tapped, about 10 minutes longer.

Carefully remove the popovers from the pan and transfer to a cooling rack. Using a paring knife, cut a small slit in the side of each popover to release some of the steam.

Serve warm with the crème fraîche, smoked salmon, capers, red onion, dill, and chives.

Although this salad is in our brunch section, it's also a favorite Sunday evening meal when served with a glass of white wine and a classic baguette. As the main feature of your breakfast, it's perfect for two, but if accompanied by other dishes at a family brunch, you can serve four to six people (just be sure to increase the number of eggs).

BISTRO BRUNCH SALAD

MAKES 2 SERVINGS

2 oz (60 g) prosciutto, thinly sliced

4 large eggs

1 teaspoon white wine vinegar

2 heads frisée (about ½ lb/225 g total weight), torn into bite-size pieces

¾ cup (6 fl oz/180 ml) Shallot-Dijon Vinaigrette (page 206), including fried shallots

Freshly ground pepper, for garnish

Crusty baguette or sourdough bread, for serving (optional)

Line a baking sheet with paper towels. In a frying pan over medium-high heat, cook the prosciutto slices until crispy, turning once, about 3 minutes. Transfer to the prepared baking sheet.

To make poached eggs, bring a saucepan half full of water to a boil. Set a small fine-mesh sieve over a bowl. Working with one at a time, crack an egg into the sieve to drain off the watery part of the white. Carefully transfer each egg to a small bowl or ramekin. Add the vinegar to the boiling water and whisk to combine. Gently slip the eggs into the water one at a time, then cover and cook for 3 minutes. Use a slotted spoon to transfer the eggs to a paper towel-lined plate to remove any water.

To assemble the salad, in a large bowl, toss the frisée with the vinaigrette until nicely coated. Add the crispy prosciutto and fried shallots and toss to combine. Transfer the salad to individual plates or a serving platter, top with the eggs, and garnish with pepper. Serve crusty bread alongside.

This smoothie, which is packed with protein, is a delicious way to add veggies to your smoothie routine. Use this recipe as inspiration for your own creations based on what you have in the fridge. For example, if you don't have or want to use a banana, substitute half an avocado, or use your favorite nut butter or hemp seeds and a little vanilla bean powder in place of the protein powder. We also like to throw in a handful of greens, like baby spinach, or sprinkle in some spirulina, moringa powder, maca powder, or matcha powder for an extra boost.

MINT CACAO CHIP SMOOTHIE

MAKES 1 SMOOTHIE

½ ripe frozen or fresh banana (see Tip)

½ cup (2 oz/60 g) frozen cauliflower rice or frozen diced zucchini

¼ cup loosely packed fresh mint leaves, including tender stems, about ½ bunch fresh mint

1 cup (8 fl oz/240 ml) plant-based milk (we like almond)

1–2 scoops vanilla or plain protein powder

Generous pinch of ground cinnamon, preferably Ceylon

1 tablespoon cacao nibs, plus more for garnish

In a blender, combine the banana, cauliflower, mint, milk, protein powder, and cinnamon. Blend on high speed until smooth. Add the cacao nibs and blend until the nibs are broken up but still have some texture (like the chocolate flecks in mint chocolate chip ice cream). Pour into a glass and garnish with more cacao nibs. Serve immediately.

TIP *If using a fresh banana, add a handful of ice.*

Not only is this smoothie pink-hued with delicious mood-lifting notes of vanilla, but it contains butterscotch-flavored maca root, an adaptogen rich in iron, potassium, and other key vitamins and minerals. This is our go-to smoothie when we want a little more pep in our step. We use our favorite vanilla-flavored collagen protein powder, which harmonizes with the strawberry flavor and, along with the cashews, creates a creamy, milk shake–like texture, but feel free to use your protein powder of choice. Aside from adding more strawberries, you can also add a little extra sweetness, like a chopped pitted Medjool date.

STRAWBERRY VANILLA MACA SMOOTHIE

MAKES 2 SMOOTHIES

Heaping ½ cup (2 oz/60 g) raw whole cashews

8 medium frozen strawberries, or to taste

1¼ cups (10 fl oz/300 ml) plant-based milk, such as almond or oat, plus more if needed to thin

1 tablespoon maca root powder

1 teaspoon vanilla bean powder

2 scoops vanilla collagen protein powder

Pinch of ground cinnamon, preferably Ceylon

6 ice cubes

Combine all of the ingredients in a blender. Blend on high speed, stopping to scrape down the sides of the blender or using the tamper, until smooth, about 1 minute.

If desired, adjust the sweetness with more strawberries or add more milk for a looser texture.

Divide between 2 glasses and serve.

SNACKS, SOUPS & SALADS

FOR THE MUHAMMARA

4 red bell peppers

3 tablespoons extra-virgin olive oil

Kosher salt

10 cloves garlic

⅔ cup (2¾ oz/80 g) toasted walnut halves

1 tablespoon dried thyme leaves

1 tablespoon balsamic vinegar

¾ teaspoon smoked paprika

¼ teaspoon red pepper flakes

Continued from previous page

Stem, quarter, and seed the bell peppers and add to a large mixing bowl. Drizzle with the oil, sprinkle with a large pinch of salt, and toss to coat evenly. Spread the pepper quarters cut side up in a single layer on the prepared baking sheet. Roast until very tender and charred, about 40 minutes. During the last 15 minutes of cooking time, add the garlic cloves to the baking sheet. Set aside to cool slightly.

Transfer the peppers and garlic to a food processor. Add the walnuts, thyme, balsamic, paprika, red pepper flakes, and 1 teaspoon salt and blend until combined, about 15 seconds for a rustic texture and 1 minute for a smooth, creamy texture. Taste and adjust the seasoning with salt. Transfer to a serving bowl and set aside to cool.

When the dough is ready, gently punch it down, then turn it out onto a lightly floured work surface. Using a bench scraper or a large knife, divide the dough into 6 equal pieces. Shape each piece into a tight ball and place on a lightly floured baking sheet. Cover loosely with plastic wrap and let rest at room temperature for 15 minutes.

Meanwhile, place a pizza stone in the upper third of the oven and preheat to 500°F (260°C). Pour the remaining 3 tablespoons oil into a small bowl and set aside.

Using a lightly floured rolling pin on a lightly floured work surface, roll a dough ball out into a 6-inch (15-cm) circle. Lightly brush the top with olive oil. If your pizza stone will hold more than 1 pita at a time, roll out a second dough ball the same way.

Swiftly place the dough round or rounds onto the heated pizza stone. Bake until the top is spotted and the bread has bubbled and cooked through, about 3 minutes. Repeat for each dough ball, keeping the baked pitas warm in a clean dish towel.

Serve the pitas alongside the herbed labneh and muhammara dips.

A batch of these crisp-tender carrots with our favorite creamy Greek ranch dip (which has been rebranded as "Granch") never lasts long in the Test Kitchen or at home. They're super easy and fun to throw together, and they make a perfect after-school snack, last-minute appetizer for friends, or side to a piece of protein for dinner. The recipe calls for an oven bake, but if you have an air fryer, air fry in batches at 400°F (200°C) for about 13 minutes.

CARROT FRIES WITH GREEK RANCH DIP

MAKES 4 SERVINGS

6 large carrots, peeled and cut into batons 4 by ½ inch (10 cm by 12 mm)

¼ cup (2 fl oz/60 ml) extra-virgin olive oil

1 cup (4 oz/115 g) grated Parmesan cheese

½ cup (1¾ oz/50 g) panko bread crumbs

2 tablespoons finely chopped fresh flat-leaf parsley leaves

Kosher salt and freshly ground pepper

Granch Dip (page 206), for serving

Position a rack in the upper third of the oven and preheat to 425°F (220°C).

In a large bowl, toss the carrots with the oil.

In a separate bowl, combine the Parmesan, panko, and parsley. Season with salt and pepper.

Sprinkle the panko mixture over the carrots and toss to coat. Transfer the carrots to a baking sheet and spread into an even layer. If there is excess panko mixture in the bowl, sprinkle it evenly over the carrots, pressing lightly to adhere.

Bake until the carrots are just cooked through and the panko is crisp, 10–15 minutes. Remove from the oven and let cool slightly.

Serve the carrot fries warm with the granch dip.

Halloumi, the Greek goat and sheep's milk cheese that you can sear, grill, fry, or even air fry, is a Test Kitchen favorite. It's salty, melty, and pairs nicely with both sweet and savory ingredients. Keep it simple by pan-searing it in a little butter or oil and then serving it with fresh herbs, flake salt, and pepper. Or get a little fancy and drizzle with our hot honey or olive-jalapeño salsa verde for an out-of-this-world appetizer you will make again and again and again.

PANFRIED HALLOUMI, TWO WAYS

MAKES 2–4 SERVINGS

1 tablespoon neutral oil, such as avocado

1 tablespoon unsalted butter

9 oz (250 g) halloumi, cut into 8 slices ½ inch (12 mm) thick

Hot Honey (page 208), for serving (optional)

Olive-Jalapeño Salsa Verde (page 209), for serving (optional)

Flake salt and coarsely ground pepper, for garnish

Chopped fresh flat-leaf parsley, for garnish

In a nonstick frying pan over medium heat, warm the oil and butter, swirling the pan to coat it evenly. Add the halloumi and cook, turning once, until golden brown and crispy, 4–6 minutes.

Arrange the halloumi slices on a warmed platter.

If desired, while the cheese is hot, liberally drizzle with the hot honey or spoon the salsa verde over the top. Garnish with salt, pepper, and parsley and serve immediately.

Concha has been a member of Devon's family for over twenty years and is known for her amazing guacamole made with fresh avocados from her tree. Below is what Devon believes is Concha's recipe, though Concha always says the same thing: there are no actual measurements, it's just by taste. Personalize with whatever you have in your kitchen, such as white onion or shallot in place of the red onion, lemon juice for the lime juice, or by omitting the chile and tomato. The key here is to use the best produce available.

CONCHA'S GUACAMOLE

MAKES 4–6 SERVINGS

5 ripe avocados, peeled, pitted, and cut into chunks

1 large ripe Roma tomato, seeded and finely diced (about ¾ cup/ 5½ oz/155 g), optional

1 serrano or jalapeño chile, seeded and finely diced (optional)

¼ cup (1¼ oz/35 g) finely chopped red onion

¼ cup (½ oz/15 g) chopped fresh cilantro

2 cloves garlic, minced

Juice of 1 lime, plus more as needed

Kosher salt

Tortilla chips, for serving

In a bowl, combine the avocados, tomato (if using), chile (if using), onion, cilantro, garlic, lime juice, and 1½ teaspoons salt. Using a wooden spoon or a large fork, mash the avocado to your desired texture.

Taste and adjust the seasoning with more salt or lime juice if needed. Serve with chips alongside for dipping.

You know what they say about chicken soup: not much beats it if you are feeling under the weather. If you like more vegetables than chicken meat or vice versa, adjust the ratio to taste. At the end of the day, the secret to any great soup is using a well-made stock. This is the time to bust out the homemade stuff—or to splurge on some high-quality stock at the store.

THE COZIEST CHICKEN NOODLE SOUP

MAKES 4 SERVINGS

2 tablespoons extra-virgin olive oil

2 medium carrots, peeled and cut on the diagonal into 1-inch (2.5-cm) pieces

2 thin celery stalks, cut into slices ¼ inch (6 mm) thick

2 medium leeks, white part only, halved and cut crosswise into slices ¼ inch (6 mm) thick

6 cups (48 fl oz/1.4 l) chicken stock, homemade (page 203) or purchased

1 bay leaf

2 fresh thyme sprigs, or ¼ teaspoon dried thyme

2 cups (12 oz/340 g) cooked shredded chicken

6 oz (170 g) dried extra-wide egg noodles

Kosher salt and freshly ground pepper

¼ cup (½ oz/15 g) minced fresh flat-leaf parsley leaves, for garnish

1 lemon, cut into wedges, for serving

In a large Dutch oven or saucepan over medium heat, warm the olive oil. When it is hot and shimmering, add the carrots and cook, stirring occasionally, until softened, about 4 minutes. Add the celery and leeks and cook, stirring occasionally, until softened, about 5 minutes.

Pour in the stock and add the bay leaf, thyme, and shredded chicken. Bring to a boil over medium-high heat, then reduce the heat to medium. Add the noodles, stir well to combine, and cook just until the noodles are tender, about 6 minutes, or according to the package instructions.

Remove and discard the bay leaf and thyme sprigs from the soup. Season with salt and pepper. Ladle the soup into warmed bowls, dividing it evenly. Garnish with the parsley and serve immediately, accompanied by the lemon wedges.

If you are going to master any soup at home, French onion, a hallmark of French cuisine, is the one. It's simply iconic. Low- and slow-cooking is the key to caramelizing the onions to melty perfection, so don't rush the process! We love to serve this soup as a main with a side salad of lightly dressed frisée or as a first course before a nice, hearty main like roast chicken or *steak frites*.

CLASSIC FRENCH ONION SOUP

MAKES 8 SERVINGS

2 tablespoons unsalted butter

2½ lb (1.1 kg) yellow onions, halved and thinly sliced

1 tablespoon all-purpose flour

1 cup (8 fl oz/240 ml) dry white wine

2 qt (1.9 l) good-quality beef stock

2 teaspoons minced fresh thyme, or 1 teaspoon dried thyme

1 bay leaf

Kosher salt and freshly ground pepper

1 crusty baguette

2⅔ cups (11 oz/310 g) shredded Gruyère cheese

In a large Dutch oven over medium heat, melt the butter. Add the onions, stir well, cover, and cook for 5 minutes. Uncover, reduce the heat to medium-low, and cook, stirring occasionally, until the onions are tender and deep golden brown, about 30 minutes.

Sprinkle the flour over the onions and stir until combined. Gradually stir in the wine, then the stock, and finally the thyme and bay leaf. Bring to a boil over high heat, reduce the heat to medium-low, and simmer, uncovered, until slightly reduced, about 30 minutes. Season with salt and pepper. Discard the bay leaf.

While the soup simmers, preheat the broiler. Have ready eight 1½-cup (12-fl oz/350-ml) broiler-proof soup crocks or ramekins, arranging them on a baking sheet. Cut the baguette into 16 slices, sizing them so that 2 slices will fit inside each crock. Arrange the bread slices on a separate baking sheet and broil, turning once, until lightly toasted on both sides, about 1 minute total. Set the slices aside. Position the oven rack about 12 inches (30 cm) from the heat source and leave the broiler on.

Ladle the hot soup into the crocks. Place 2 toasted bread slices, overlapping if necessary, on top of the soup and sprinkle each crock evenly with about ⅓ cup (1½ oz/40 g) of the Gruyère. Broil until the cheese is bubbling, about 2 minutes. Serve immediately.

Who doesn't love the childhood comfort of tomato soup with grilled cheese? Well, we've taken this nostalgic dish into adulthood and created an elevated version without compromising the simplicity. If you cannot find sliced Muenster, swap in whatever melty cheese you love: American, mozzarella, and Cheddar are some of our favorites, but Colby, Monterey Jack, and Havarti are excellent options as well.

TOMATO SOUP WITH MUENSTER CROUTONS

MAKES 6 SERVINGS

FOR THE TOMATO SOUP
4 tablespoons (2 oz/60 g) unsalted butter

1 yellow onion, diced

4 cloves garlic, smashed

1 tablespoon sugar

½ teaspoon celery seeds, plus more for serving

Kosher salt and freshly ground pepper

2 cans (each 28 oz/800 g) whole San Marzano tomatoes with juices

1 cup (8 fl oz/240 ml) vegetable stock or chicken stock, homemade (page 203) or purchased

¾ cup (6 fl oz/180 ml) heavy cream

Flake salt, for serving

FOR THE MUENSTER CROUTONS
4 tablespoons (2 oz/60 g) unsalted butter, at room temperature

4 slices sourdough bread, each about ½ inch (12 mm) thick

4½ oz (130 g) sliced Muenster cheese

To make the soup, in a large saucepan over medium heat, melt the butter. Add the onion and cook, stirring, until tender but not browned, about 10 minutes. Add the garlic and cook, stirring, until softened and fragrant, about 2 minutes. Add the sugar and celery seeds, then season with kosher salt and pepper, stirring to combine.

Add the tomatoes, crushing them with your hands as you add them. Add their juices and the stock and bring to a boil over medium-high heat, stirring occasionally and breaking up the tomatoes with a wooden spoon. Reduce the heat to medium-low and simmer, stirring occasionally, for about 10 minutes. Remove from the heat and set aside to cool for about 5 minutes.

Transfer the soup to a blender and blend on high speed until smooth. Return to the saucepan, add the cream, and stir until combined. Season with kosher salt and pepper. Cover and keep warm over low heat.

To make the Muenster croutons, spread butter on one side of each bread slice. Preheat a large nonstick frying pan over medium-high heat. Place 2 slices of the bread, butter side down, in the frying pan, then divide the cheese evenly between the slices. Top with the remaining bread slices, butter side up. Cover and cook, turning once, until the bread is golden brown on both sides and the cheese is melted, about 4 minutes.

Transfer to a cutting board and let rest for 5 minutes to set, then use a serrated knife to cut into approximately 1-inch (2.5-cm) squares.

Divide the warm soup among warmed bowls and top with a light sprinkle of celery seeds, a pinch of flake salt, and a few croutons. Serve immediately.

Here is the perfect fall soup. Crispy, buttery croutons add textural contrast to the velvety butternut squash purée, and an Italian-inspired gremolata made with toasted hazelnuts lends a bright, refreshing note. The soup, croutons, and gremolata can all be made up to 2 days in advance (just reheat the soup gently in a saucepan), but wait until just before serving to combine them.

BUTTERNUT SQUASH SOUP WITH HAZELNUT GREMOLATA

MAKES 4 SERVINGS

FOR THE BROWN BUTTER CROUTONS
1 small loaf crusty sourdough bread, about ¾ lb (340 g), torn into 1-inch (2.5-cm) pieces

½ cup (4 oz/115 g) unsalted butter

Kosher salt

FOR THE BUTTERNUT SQUASH SOUP
2 large butternut squashes, each 1½–2 lb (680 g–1 kg)

6 tablespoons (3 oz/90 g) unsalted butter

2 yellow onions, chopped

4 fresh sage leaves, chopped, plus leaves for garnish (optional)

6 cups (48 fl oz/1.4 l) chicken stock or vegetable stock, homemade (page 203) or purchased

Kosher salt and freshly ground pepper

Pinch of freshly grated nutmeg (optional)

Pinch of sugar (optional)

To make the croutons, preheat the oven to 325°F (165°C). Place the bread in a heatproof bowl. In a small frying pan over medium heat, melt the butter. Reduce the heat to medium-low and cook, stirring frequently, until the butter is toasty brown and smells nutty, about 5 minutes, watching the butter carefully at the end to make sure it doesn't burn. Pour the butter over the bread and toss until evenly coated. Season with ⅛ teaspoon salt.

Spread the bread into an even layer on a baking sheet. Bake, tossing the bread pieces once halfway through, until the croutons are light golden brown, about 20 minutes. The croutons should be crisp on the edges but still give a little when pinched with your fingers. Taste and season with more salt if desired. Set aside. (The croutons can be stored, covered, at room temperature for up to 2 days.)

Increase the oven temperature to 400°F (200°C).

To make the soup, prick each squash several times with the tip of a knife. Place the whole squashes on a baking sheet and roast until they feel somewhat soft to the touch and a knife penetrates the skin easily, about 1 hour. Remove from the oven and, when cool enough to handle, cut in half lengthwise and remove and discard the seeds and fibers. Scoop out the pulp into a bowl and set aside.

While the squash is roasting, make the gremolata. In a food processor, combine the parsley, hazelnuts, lemon zest, and garlic. Pulse until the hazelnuts are about the size of sunflower seeds, the parsley is minced, and the mixture is just combined. Transfer to a bowl. Stir in the lemon juice and enough olive oil to make a thick sauce. Season

FOR THE HAZELNUT GREMOLATA

1 cup (2 oz/60 g) fresh flat-leaf parsley leaves

⅓ cup (1⅔ oz/45 g) chopped toasted hazelnuts

Finely grated zest and juice of 1 lemon

2 cloves garlic, minced

Extra-virgin olive oil

Kosher salt

with salt. Set aside, or cover and refrigerate until ready to use, up to 2 days.

To finish the soup, in a saucepan over low heat, melt the butter. Add the onions and chopped sage and cook, stirring occasionally, until the onions are tender and translucent, 8–10 minutes. Add the stock and squash, raise the heat to high, and bring to a boil. Reduce the heat to low and simmer for a few minutes to combine the flavors. Remove from the heat.

Working in batches, purée the soup in a blender or food processor. Return to a clean saucepan. Alternatively, use an immersion blender, then pass the soup through a food mill placed over the pan. Reheat gently over medium-low heat. Season with salt and pepper. Taste the soup and add the nutmeg and sugar if a little more sweetness is desired.

Ladle into warmed bowls and top with the croutons and gremolata, dividing them evenly. Garnish with additional sage leaves if desired, and serve immediately.

Vichyssoise is a thick and flavorful French soup traditionally made with potatoes, leeks, and cream. In our version, we swap out the potatoes for cauliflower and omit the cream in favor of a high-powered blender for a lighter, more modern twist on the classic. Eat this soup warm or at room temperature, or even chilled like the French do. The crispy prosciutto takes the soup to the next level, but you can omit it to make this a vegetarian dish.

CAULIFLOWER VICHYSSOISE WITH CRISPY PROSCIUTTO

MAKES 4-6 SERVINGS

1 large head cauliflower, cored and cut into 1-inch (2.5-cm) pieces

2 shallots, quartered

4 cloves garlic

¼ cup (2 fl oz/60 ml) plus 3 tablespoons extra-virgin olive oil, plus more for serving

Kosher salt and freshly ground pepper

3 oz (90 g) prosciutto (about 6 thin slices)

4 cups (32 fl oz/950 ml) chicken stock or vegetable stock, homemade (page 203) or purchased

½ cup (2 oz/60 g) grated Parmesan cheese, plus more for serving (optional)

Preheat the oven to 400°F (200°C).

Arrange the cauliflower, shallots, and garlic on a rimmed baking sheet and drizzle with ¼ cup (2 fl oz/60 ml) of the oil. Season generously with salt and pepper. Toss to coat. Roast until the cauliflower is tender and lightly browned, 30–35 minutes.

Meanwhile, make the crispy prosciutto. Line another rimmed baking sheet with parchment paper. Arrange the prosciutto slices on the baking sheet, bunching up the slices slightly so they do not lie completely flat and making sure they do not touch. Bake until the slices begin to shrivel and brown, 10–12 minutes. Remove from the oven and allow to cool on the baking sheet; the prosciutto will crisp as it cools.

In a large saucepan over medium heat, warm the stock. Transfer to a blender along with the roasted cauliflower mixture and Parmesan.

Blend on high speed until very smooth and creamy. With the blender running, slowly add the remaining 3 tablespoons oil, blending for about 1½ minutes; the soup will be extremely light and fluffy.

Divide the soup among warmed bowls and top with a drizzle of olive oil, a sprinkle of Parmesan (if using), a piece of the prosciutto, and some pepper. Serve immediately.

What we love about minestrone is that it is as comforting and hearty as it is fresh and light. Our version, packed with cannellini beans, gets its richness from the sausage and Parmesan and its freshness from the dino kale and a big ol' squeeze of lemon juice. To make this soup vegetarian, simply omit the sausage and follow the recipe as written.

SAUSAGE AND KALE MINESTRONE

MAKES 2–4 SERVINGS

5 tablespoons (2½ fl oz/75 ml) extra-virgin olive oil

½ lb (225 g) mild Italian sausage, casings removed

1 yellow onion, diced

2 carrots, peeled and coarsely diced

1 celery stalk, diced

2 cloves garlic, minced

2 cans (each 14 oz/400 g) cannellini beans, drained and rinsed

4 cups (32 fl oz/950 ml) chicken stock, homemade (page 203) or purchased

1 cup (4 oz/115 g) grated Parmesan cheese

2 fresh rosemary sprigs

Juice of ½ lemon

1 small baguette, cut on the diagonal into slices ½ inch (12 mm) thick

Kosher salt and freshly ground pepper

2 bunches dinosaur kale, stems removed and leaves chopped

In a Dutch oven or heavy pot over medium heat, warm 3 tablespoons of the oil. Crumble the sausage into the pot and cook, breaking it into pieces with a wooden spoon, until browned, about 7 minutes. Add the onion, carrots, celery, and garlic and cook, stirring occasionally, until the vegetables are tender, about 5 minutes. Add the beans and stock and bring to a boil. Reduce the heat to medium-low and add ½ cup (2 oz/60 g) of the Parmesan, the rosemary sprigs, and lemon juice. Cover the pot and simmer, stirring occasionally, for about 30 minutes.

Meanwhile, preheat the oven to 375°F (190°C).

Brush the baguette slices on both sides with the remaining 2 tablespoons oil and season lightly with salt. Arrange on a baking sheet in a single layer. Bake, turning once halfway through, until the bread is golden brown and toasted, about 10 minutes. Remove from the oven and let cool slightly.

While the crostini are cooling, remove the rosemary sprigs from the soup. Add the kale and cook, stirring occasionally, until the kale is wilted and tender but still bright green, about 5 minutes. Taste the soup and season with salt and pepper.

To serve, ladle the soup into individual bowls and serve with the crostini and the remaining ½ cup (2 oz/55 g) Parmesan.

Seeking a fresh take on classic lobster bisque, we set out to create a dairy-free (but equally decadent) version. Creamy coconut milk turned out to be the solution and, in turn, inspired the inclusion of flavors like lemongrass and ginger. The key to rich lobster flavor and overall depth is starting with homemade lobster stock—here, enriched with lemongrass—which can sometimes be a lengthy, complicated process. But we simplified it enough that you can have a delicious bisque within an hour. And we promise, making your own stock here is 100 percent worth it.

LEMONGRASS LOBSTER BISQUE WITH COCONUT MILK

MAKES 4 SERVINGS

FOR THE LOBSTER STOCK
7 cups (56 fl oz/1.7 l) water

Kosher salt

5 lobster tails, each 3–4 oz (90–115 g), thawed if frozen

2 bay leaves

½ yellow onion (with stem intact)

2 lemongrass stalks (bulb portion only), each 4 inches (10 cm) long, halved lengthwise

FOR THE BISQUE
¼ cup (2 fl oz/60 ml) extra-virgin olive oil

1 large yellow onion, diced

5 cloves garlic, minced

3 tablespoons minced fresh lemongrass, tender bulb portion only

One 3-inch (7.5-cm) piece fresh ginger, peeled and grated (about 1½ tablespoons)

¼ cup (2 oz/60 g) tomato paste

¼ cup (2 fl oz/60 ml) mirin

1 tablespoon arrowroot powder (or cornstarch)

Kosher salt

3 cans (each 13½ fl oz/400 ml) unsweetened coconut milk

1 tablespoon coconut sugar, or more to taste (optional)

Juice of 1 lime, plus more if needed

To make the lobster stock, have ready a large bowl of ice water. In a large soup pot over high heat, combine the 7 cups (56 fl oz/1.7 l) water and 2 teaspoons salt and bring to a boil. Add the lobster tails, bay leaves, onion, and lemongrass stalks, cover, and cook until the lobster tails turn bright red, 4–5 minutes. Using tongs, transfer the lobster tails to the ice bath. Set the stock aside.

When cool to the touch, slice the lobster tails in half lengthwise, remove the veins, and carefully remove the meat. Transfer the meat to an airtight container and refrigerate until ready to use. Return the shells to the cooking liquid and bring the liquid back to a boil over high heat. Reduce the heat to medium-low and simmer, uncovered, until reduced by half, about 40 minutes.

Strain the stock through a fine-mesh sieve set over a large heatproof bowl, discarding the solids; you should have about 3 cups (24 fl oz/700 ml) stock. Set the stock aside.

To make the bisque, in a large Dutch oven or heavy pot over medium heat, warm the oil. Add the onion and cook, stirring occasionally, until translucent, about 5 minutes. Add the garlic, lemongrass, and ginger and cook, stirring, until fragrant, about 2 minutes. Stir in the tomato paste until distributed and cook, stirring, until slightly caramelized, about 2 minutes. Deglaze the pot with the mirin, scraping up any bits stuck to the bottom of the pot and cooking until the liquid is absorbed, about 1 minute. Sprinkle in the arrowroot and 2 teaspoons salt. Stir to combine.

FOR THE GARNISH

5 green onions, thinly sliced
on the diagonal

3 tablespoons finely chopped
fresh chives

Leaves from ½ bunch fresh cilantro

Add 2 cans of the coconut milk. Scrape out the solid coconut cream from the third can and add to the bisque, discarding the liquid coconut water. Add the 3 cups (24 fl oz/700 ml) reserved lobster stock and whisk to combine. Bring to a boil over high heat, then reduce the heat to medium and simmer, uncovered, until reduced slightly, about 10 minutes.

Using an immersion blender, blend the bisque until smooth. Season with salt, then add the coconut sugar (if using) and lime juice. Taste and add more lime juice if desired.

Chop half of the lobster meat into bite-size pieces and add to the bisque. Reserve the remaining half tails for serving. Simmer the bisque gently over medium heat just until the lobster meat is heated through.

Ladle the bisque into bowls. Top each bowl with a reserved halved tail, then garnish with the green onions, chives, and cilantro. Serve immediately.

Lemongrass Lobster
Bisque with Coconut
Milk, page 72

Salmon Niçoise Salad with Charred Green Onion Pesto, page 76

First, we think we can all agree that this is the most beautiful salad on the planet. Second, it is perhaps one of the most delicious. Our modern take on the classic Provençal niçoise salad swaps out the tuna for Dijon mustard–roasted salmon and a charred green onion pesto for the vinaigrette. The green onions are charred in a cast-iron pan over high heat, then blended with anchovies, capers, garlic, olive oil, and plenty of fresh herbs for brightness.

SALMON NIÇOISE SALAD WITH CHARRED GREEN ONION PESTO

MAKES 4 SERVINGS

FOR THE CHARRED GREEN ONION PESTO

12 green onions, white and pale green parts

1 tablespoon neutral oil, such as canola or avocado

2 cups (2 oz/60 g) packed fresh basil leaves

½ cup (1 oz/30 g) packed fresh flat-leaf parsley leaves

4 oil-cured anchovy fillets, roughly chopped

1 tablespoon capers

1 clove garlic, chopped

⅔ cup (5½ fl oz/160 ml) extra-virgin olive oil

2 tablespoons white wine vinegar

Kosher salt and freshly ground pepper

FOR THE SALMON

1½ lb (680 g) center-cut skinless salmon fillet

1 tablespoon Dijon mustard

Kosher salt and freshly ground pepper

1 tablespoon extra-virgin olive oil

Preheat the oven to 400°F (200°C).

To make the pesto, heat a cast-iron frying pan over high heat. Add the green onions and cook, turning occasionally, until charred and softened, about 10 minutes, adding the neutral oil halfway through cooking. Transfer to a cutting board and trim the ends. Roughly chop the green onions, then transfer to a food processor. Add the basil, parsley, anchovies, capers, and garlic and pulse until finely chopped and blended. Continue to pulse while slowly adding the olive oil and vinegar through the feed tube, then process until smooth. Season to taste with salt and pepper. Set aside.

To make the salmon, pat the salmon dry with paper towels. Place on a rimmed baking sheet and brush with the mustard. Season with salt and pepper, then drizzle with the olive oil. Roast until the salmon is opaque throughout, about 13 minutes for medium. Set aside.

Meanwhile, start on the salad. Add the potatoes to a large pot of cold salted water and bring to a boil over high heat. Cook until fork-tender, 8–15 minutes, depending on their size. Using a slotted spoon, transfer the potatoes to a large bowl; keep the water boiling for the green beans. Add the olive oil to the potatoes, season with salt and pepper, and toss to coat; set aside.

FOR THE SALAD

1 lb (450 g) fingerling potatoes

Kosher salt and freshly ground pepper

1 tablespoon extra-virgin olive oil

¾ lb (340 g) green beans, trimmed

Juice of ½ lemon

4 large eggs

1 head Little Gem lettuce,
leaves separated

¾ cup (3¾ oz/110 g) assorted olives

6 radishes, stems intact
and halved lengthwise

1 avocado, pitted, peeled,
and thinly sliced

Flake salt

Have ready a large bowl of ice water. Add the green beans to the boiling water and cook until crisp-tender, about 3 minutes. Using a slotted spoon, transfer the beans to the ice water to stop the cooking; keep the water boiling for the eggs. Drain the beans, transfer to a medium bowl, and toss with the lemon juice and a pinch of salt; set aside.

Have ready a bowl of cold water. Add the eggs to the boiling water and cook for 6 minutes. Drain and transfer to the cold water. When cool enough to handle, peel the eggs and cut in half lengthwise.

Arrange the lettuce on a serving platter. Break the salmon into large chunks, then arrange on the platter along with the three-quarters, green beans, eggs, olives, radishes, and avocado. Season the eggs and avocado with flake salt and pepper. Serve the charred green onion pesto alongside.

Our version of bouillabaisse, the classic Provençal stew, is brimming with a variety of seafood in a richly seasoned tomato base. And though it's a lengthy process, we promise that making your own fish stock will transport you from your kitchen at home to a quaint bistro in France. Just ask your fishmonger for fish bones, heads, and bodies to make it. PS: The slices of toasted baguette slathered with garlicky aioli are not only a serving suggestion but a requirement for soaking up all the deliciousness.

BOUILLABAISSE WITH GARLIC AIOLI TOASTS

MAKES 4-6 SERVINGS

FOR THE BOUILLABAISSE
½ cup (4 fl oz/120 ml)
extra-virgin olive oil

1 large yellow onion, diced

1 fennel bulb, trimmed, cored, and
diced, fronds reserved for garnish

4 cloves garlic, minced

½ teaspoon saffron threads, crumbled

Kosher salt and freshly ground pepper

5 cups (40 fl oz/1.2 l) fish stock,
homemade (page 204) or purchased

1 can (28 oz/800 g) diced tomatoes
with juices

½ lb (225 g) skinless halibut or other
flaky white fish fillet, cut into 1-inch
(2.5-cm) pieces

1 lb (450 g) mussels, scrubbed
and debearded

1 lb (450 g) small clams, scrubbed

½ lb (225 g) medium shrimp, peeled
and deveined, with tails intact

½ lb (225 g) sea scallops, quartered

FOR THE GARLIC AIOLI TOASTS
½ baguette, cut on the diagonal
into slices ¼ inch (6 mm) thick

Extra-virgin olive oil

Garlic Aioli (page 212)

Lemon wedges, for serving

To make the bouillabaisse, in a large Dutch oven over medium-high heat, warm the olive oil. Add the onion and fennel bulb and cook, stirring occasionally, until softened and starting to brown, about 8 minutes. Add the garlic and saffron and cook, stirring occasionally, until fragrant, about 1 minute. Season with salt.

Reduce the heat to medium-low and stir in the stock and tomatoes with their juices. Increase the heat to medium and bring to a simmer, then simmer vigorously for 10 minutes. Add the halibut and cook until almost opaque, about 2 minutes. Add the mussels, clams, and shrimp. Cover and cook until the mussels and clams open and the shrimp are opaque, 3-5 minutes. Add the scallops and simmer until opaque, 1-2 minutes. Discard any unopened mussels and clams. Remove from the heat and season to taste with salt and pepper.

While the soup is cooking, make the garlic aioli toasts. Position a rack in the upper third of the oven and preheat to 425°F (220°C). Place the baguette slices on a baking sheet in a single layer and drizzle generously with olive oil. Bake until lightly toasted and golden, 6-8 minutes. Spread the garlic aioli over the toasts.

Ladle the bouillabaisse into bowls and garnish with the reserved fennel fronds. Serve with the garlic aioli toasts and lemon wedges.

Another spin on a classic, our Cobb is topped with New York strip steak instead of the usual chicken and paired with bitter chicories instead of iceberg or romaine, which we think balances the creamy blue cheese beautifully. We like to add grilled corn, but if your corn is in season, feel free to keep it raw to add an extra sweet crunch. We add sliced jalapeño chile for a spicy kick, but leave it out if that's not your thing.

STEAK COBB SALAD

MAKES 4 SERVINGS

FOR THE DRESSING
1 small shallot, minced

3 tablespoons red wine vinegar

1 tablespoon Dijon mustard

½ cup (4 fl oz/120 ml)
extra-virgin olive oil

1 tablespoon minced fresh chives

Kosher salt and freshly ground pepper

FOR THE COBB SALAD
1 New York strip steak, about ½ lb (225 g)

Kosher salt and freshly ground pepper

2 tablespoons extra-virgin olive oil

1 ear of corn, shucked

1 lb (450 g) mixed chicories, such as Belgian endive, radicchio, and frisée, coarsely chopped

1½ lb (680 g) assorted heirloom tomatoes (cherry and regular), sliced

1 avocado, pitted, peeled and sliced

2 soft-cooked eggs (see Salmon Niçoise Salad, page 76), peeled and halved lengthwise

6 oz (170 g) blue cheese, cut into slices ¼ inch (6 mm) thick

1 jalapeño chile, seeded and thinly sliced crosswise

1 tablespoon minced fresh chives

To make the dressing, in a bowl, combine the shallot and vinegar. Let stand for 10 minutes, then whisk in the mustard. While whisking, slowly pour in the oil and continue to whisk until smooth. Stir in the chives and season to taste with salt and pepper. Set aside.

To make the salad, season the steak generously on both sides with salt and pepper. Let stand at room temperature for 20–30 minutes.

Meanwhile, preheat a grill pan over medium-high heat, then brush with 1 tablespoon of the oil. Add the corn and cook, turning occasionally, until charred and softened all over, about 6 minutes. Transfer to a cutting board and let cool slightly, then cut the kernels off the cob and set aside.

Brush the pan with the remaining 1 tablespoon olive oil and heat until it just starts to smoke. Add the steak and cook, turning once, until nicely browned and an instant-read thermometer inserted into the center of the meat registers 130°F (54°C), about 3 minutes per side for medium-rare, or until cooked to your liking. Transfer to a cutting board and let rest while you assemble the salad, then cut the steak into slices.

In a large bowl, toss the chicories with some of the dressing and season with salt and pepper. Arrange on a platter. Arrange the corn, tomatoes, and avocado on top of the chicories, season with salt and pepper, and drizzle with more of the dressing. Arrange the halved eggs, blue cheese, jalapeño, and steak on the salad. Garnish with the chives and several grinds of pepper. Serve immediately, passing the remaining dressing at the table.

In this springtime salad, bitter greens are tossed with sweet peas and crispy prosciutto before being topped with nutty Parmesan, resulting in a marvelous combination of contrasting flavors and textures. A creamy dressing made with rich buttermilk and sour cream ties everything together and softens the bitterness of the greens.

BITTER GREENS SALAD WITH PEAS AND PROSCIUTTO

MAKES 6 SERVINGS

FOR THE BUTTERMILK-PARMESAN DRESSING
1 cup (4 oz/115 g) grated Parmesan cheese

¾ cup (6 fl oz/180 ml) buttermilk

2 tablespoons extra-virgin olive oil

1 tablespoon white wine vinegar

Finely grated zest and juice of ½ lemon

2 cloves garlic, minced

¼ cup (2 oz/60 g) sour cream

Freshly ground pepper

Kosher salt

FOR THE SALAD
Kosher salt and freshly ground pepper

1½ cups (7½ oz/210 g) fresh or thawed frozen peas

1 tablespoon extra-virgin olive oil

¼ lb (115 g) thinly sliced prosciutto, cut into 2-inch (5-cm) pieces

4 heads Belgian endive, stemmed and quartered

1 large head radicchio, stemmed and cut into strips

3 bunches watercress, tough stems removed

1-oz (30-g) piece Parmesan cheese

To make the dressing, in a blender, combine the Parmesan, buttermilk, olive oil, vinegar, lemon zest and juice, and garlic and blend on high speed until combined, about 30 seconds. Add the sour cream and a generous amount of pepper and blend on high speed for 30 seconds. Season to taste with salt. Set aside.

To make the salad, bring a saucepan three-quarters full of salted water to a boil over high heat. Have ready a large bowl of ice water. Add the peas to the boiling water and blanch for 1 minute. Using a sieve, scoop out the peas and refresh them in the ice water. Scoop them out of the ice water with the sieve and set aside.

In a frying pan over medium-high heat, warm the oil. Add the prosciutto and cook, stirring frequently, until crisp, about 5 minutes. Transfer to a paper towel–lined plate.

In a large bowl, combine the endive, radicchio, watercress, and reserved peas. Add the prosciutto and dressing and toss to coat. Shave the cheese over the salad and season generously with pepper. Serve immediately.

A "chopped" salad is exactly that: all the ingredients have been chopped to be roughly the same size. This recipe includes many Test Kitchen favorites in perfect balance. Buttery Roquefort, crisp bacon, red onion, radicchio, and a trio of chopped greens add texture and a touch of saltiness, while pickled beets, lemon juice, and vinegar provide tang, and honey and tomato deliver a delicious savory-sweet bite.

THE TEST KITCHEN CHOPPED SALAD

MAKES 4–6 SERVINGS

FOR THE DRESSING

½ cup (4 fl oz/120 ml) extra-virgin olive oil

1 cup (4¾ oz/135 g) crumbled blue cheese, such as Roquefort or Danish Blue Cheese

3 tablespoons champagne or white wine vinegar

2 tablespoons fresh lemon juice

1 teaspoon honey, preferably local wildflower honey

Kosher salt and freshly ground pepper

FOR THE SALAD

10 oz (285 g) thick-sliced applewood-smoked bacon

4 cups (7 oz/200 g) roughly chopped baby kale

4 cups (7 oz/200 g) roughly chopped romaine lettuce

2 cups (3½ oz/100 g) roughly chopped radicchio

1 small red onion, halved and thinly sliced

1 can (14 oz/400 g) hearts of palm, drained and quartered

1 cup (6 oz/170 g) halved cherry tomatoes

1 cup (7 oz/200 g) thinly sliced pickled beets

To make the dressing, in a food processor or blender, combine the olive oil, half of the blue cheese, the vinegar, lemon juice, honey, ½ teaspoon salt, and ½ teaspoon pepper and blend until smooth. Transfer to a bowl and refrigerate until ready to serve. (The dressing can be kept in an airtight container in the refrigerator for up to 5 days.)

Preheat the oven to 400°F (200°C).

To make the salad, line a large rimmed baking sheet with parchment paper. Arrange the bacon in a single layer on the prepared baking sheet. Bake until crisp, 18–20 minutes. Line a plate with a paper towel and set aside.

Meanwhile, in a large bowl, combine the kale, romaine, radicchio, red onion, hearts of palm, and tomatoes. Set aside.

When the bacon is crisp, transfer to the paper towel-lined plate to drain and cool. When cool enough to handle, chop the bacon into bite-size pieces. Add three-quarters of the bacon to the salad.

Toss the salad with ½ cup (4 fl oz/120 ml) of the dressing until evenly coated; taste and add more if desired. Gently fold the beets into the salad. Transfer to a serving platter. Garnish the salad with the remaining blue cheese, the remaining bacon, and a few grinds of pepper. Serve immediately.

TIP *For an additional crunchy topping, add the fried shallots from Lena's Chili Crisp (page 210).*

This dish, inspired by Belle's dad (a corn nut junkie), is a hybrid of a lot of favorite bites. Big roasted broccoli, classic Caesar dressing, and the iconic road trip/bar snack come together to create a whole new and delicious way to eat your greens. It's rich in flavor and a little playful in spirit. Serve this dish in place of a green salad and add a piece of protein like steak, fish, or chicken for a well-rounded meal.

ROASTED BROCCOLI CAESAR WITH CORN NUTS

MAKES 6–8 SERVINGS

FOR THE CAESAR DRESSING
4 oil-cured anchovy fillets

5 cloves garlic

1 large egg plus 2 large egg yolks

Finely grated zest and juice of 1 lemon

1 tablespoon Dijon mustard

1 cup (8 fl oz/240 ml) neutral oil, such as canola

2 tablespoons extra-virgin olive oil

¼ cup (1 oz/30 g) grated Parmesan cheese

Kosher salt and freshly ground pepper

FOR THE ROASTED BROCCOLI
4 heads broccoli, cut into 6 large pieces (including stems)

Extra-virgin olive oil

Freshly ground pepper

½ cup (1⅔ oz/45 g) corn nuts, lightly crushed, for garnish

1 oz (30 g) Parmesan cheese, shaved, for garnish

1 lemon, quartered, for serving

Preheat the oven to 475°F (245°C).

To make the dressing, in a blender, combine the anchovies, garlic, whole egg and egg yolks, lemon zest and juice, mustard, and a splash of water and blend until well mixed. With the blender running, slowly pour in the neutral oil to make a thick dressing. Add the olive oil, Parmesan, and salt and pepper to taste and blend until thoroughly combined.

To roast the broccoli, in a medium bowl, using tongs, toss the broccoli with ½ cup (4 fl oz/120 ml) of the dressing, 1 tablespoon olive oil, and some pepper until coated. Spread the broccoli out on a baking sheet and roast until the broccoli is charred and tender, 16–18 minutes.

To serve, place the broccoli on a serving platter and drizzle more dressing over the top. (If desired, thin out the dressing with 2–3 teaspoons water or lemon juice.) Garnish with the crushed corn nuts, shaved Parmesan, and lemon wedges.

Celebrating both the citrus of Northern California and avocado, a staple of the Californian diet, this salad combines the two for a refreshing, gorgeous dish. As we say in the Test Kitchen, an avocado is only as good as its ripeness. So to check if an avocado is at its prime, remove the small cap at the top of the avocado—it should pull away easily and be green underneath. You can keep an avocado from oxidizing (browning) by rubbing the cut side with lemon or lime juice and leaving in the pit, but it's best to cut avocados as close to serving time as possible.

NORCAL CITRUS AND AVOCADO SALAD

MAKES 6 SERVINGS

8 assorted citrus fruits, such as Cara Cara oranges, blood oranges, navel oranges, and/or small pink grapefruits

3 avocados, peeled, pitted, and sliced

¼ cup (1 oz/30 g) toasted pistachios, roughly chopped

Extra-virgin olive oil

Flake salt and freshly ground pepper

Assorted tender herbs, fennel fronds, edible flowers, and/or micro arugula, for garnish

Using a sharp knife, cut a thin slice off both ends of each citrus fruit, then cut away the peel and bitter white pith, following the fruit's curve. Slice each fruit crosswise into rounds ¼ inch (6 mm) thick.

Arrange the citrus on a serving platter with the avocado slices. Sprinkle with the pistachios, drizzle with the olive oil, and then garnish with the salt, pepper, and herbs. Serve immediately.

PIZZA, PASTA
& BREADS

Unlike Neapolitan pizza, which is famous for its thin and blistery crust, Sicilian style is a thick-crust rectangular pizza more like focaccia. The Italian name for it, *sfincione*, translates to "thick sponge," which, if you ask us, is the perfect texture to soak up all that delicious tomato sauce and cheese. All that is to say, if you love crust like we love crust, this is the pizza for you.

SHEET PAN PIZZA, SICILIAN-STYLE

MAKES ONE 13-BY-9-INCH (33-BY-23-CM) PIZZA; 2-4 SERVINGS

Neutral oil, such as avocado or canola

1 lb (450 g) pizza dough, homemade (page 205) or purchased

½ cup (4 fl oz/120 ml) Belle's Pomodoro Sauce (page 204) or your favorite tomato-based pizza sauce, plus more for dipping

1 lb (450 g) fresh mozzarella cheese, cut into slices ¼ inch (6 mm) thick

1 cup (4 oz/115 g) freshly grated pecorino romano cheese

Freshly grated Parmesan cheese, for garnish

Red pepper flakes, for garnish (optional)

Position a rack in the lower third of the oven and preheat to 500°F (260°C).

Lightly coat the bottom and sides of a 13-by-9-inch (33-by-23-cm) rimmed baking sheet with 1 tablespoon oil. Using lightly oiled hands, gently stretch the dough out to the edges and corners of the pan. If the dough springs back toward the center, cover it with plastic wrap and let stand for 10 minutes, then repeat to stretch the dough until it fills the pan.

Top the dough evenly with the sauce, leaving a border ½-1 inch (12 mm-2.5 cm) wide, then arrange the mozzarella and pecorino evenly over the top. Bake until the edges are golden brown and the sauce and cheese are bubbling, 18-20 minutes.

Let cool for 2-3 minutes, then transfer the pizza to a large cutting board. Generously cover the pizza crust with Parmesan, then sprinkle the entire pizza with red pepper flakes if desired. Serve immediately, passing more sauce for dipping.

This pie, inspired by that late-night pizza craving, is meant to be devoured with friends. Both the dough and pomodoro sauce can be made ahead, which makes this an easy, shareable dish that can be thrown together and baked in under an hour. We recommend you grab a gutsy red wine to stand up to the flavors of the sausage, pomodoro sauce, and delicious hot honey, but if we're talking *really* late-night 'za, save the bottle and stick with the boxed wine—and/or a tall glass of water.

LATE-NIGHT 'ZA WITH HOT HONEY AND PICKLED JALAPEÑOS

MAKES ONE 13-BY-18-INCH (33-BY-45-CM) PIZZA; 2-4 SERVINGS

Extra-virgin olive oil

¼ lb (115 g) mild or hot Italian sausage, casings removed

1 lb (450 g) pizza dough, homemade (page 205) or purchased

½ cup (4 fl oz/120 ml) Belle's Pomodoro Sauce (page 204) or your favorite tomato-based pizza sauce

¼ lb (115 g) fresh mozzarella cheese, cut into slices ¼ inch (6 mm) thick

2 oz (55 g) mini pepperoni

2 tablespoons Hot Honey (page 208)

Pickled jalapeños, for garnish (optional)

In a frying pan over medium heat, warm 1 tablespoon oil. Crumble the sausage into the pan and cook, stirring, until browned and cooked through, 3-5 minutes. Set aside.

Position a rack in the lower third of the oven and preheat to 500°F (260°C).

Lightly coat the bottom and sides of a 13-by-18-inch (33-by-45-cm) rimmed baking sheet with 1 tablespoon oil. Using lightly oiled hands, gently stretch the dough out to the edges and corners of the pan. If the dough springs back toward the center, cover it with plastic wrap and let stand for 10 minutes, then repeat to stretch the dough until it fills the pan.

Top the dough evenly with the sauce, then arrange the mozzarella, sausage, and pepperoni evenly over the top. Bake until the edges are golden brown and the sauce and cheese are bubbling, 18-20 minutes.

Let cool for 2-3 minutes, then transfer the pizza to a large cutting board. Drizzle the pizza with the honey, then top with pickled jalapeños if desired. Serve immediately.

Topped with artichokes, Castelvetrano olives, two kinds of cheese, and fresh and dried oregano, this pizza is packed with flavor. To streamline the prep, we call for canned artichokes, which we first roast until nicely crisped and then arrange on the pie. You can bake your pizza in a conventional oven or, if you have one, in a pizza oven following the manufacturer's instructions. If using a pizza oven, you'll still need to roast the artichokes in a regular oven first for ideal crispiness.

ROASTED ARTICHOKE PIZZA WITH CASTELVETRANO OLIVES AND OREGANO

MAKES TWO 12-INCH (30-CM) PIZZAS; 4-8 SERVINGS

1 can (15 oz/425 g) water-packed artichoke hearts, drained and patted dry

¼ cup (2 fl oz/60 ml) extra-virgin olive oil

Kosher salt and freshly ground black pepper

1 lb (450 g) pizza dough, homemade (page 205) or purchased

All-purpose flour, for dusting

1 cup (8 fl oz/240 ml) Belle's Pomodoro Sauce (page 204) or your favorite tomato-based pizza sauce

2 cups (8 oz/225 g) shredded mozzarella cheese

½ cup (4 oz/115 g) whole-milk ricotta cheese

2 teaspoons dried oregano

⅔ cup (3 oz/80 g) Castelvetrano olives, pitted and halved

Red pepper flakes, for garnish

Fresh oregano sprigs, for garnish

Position a rack in the upper third of the oven and preheat to 400°F (200°C).

On a baking sheet, toss the artichoke hearts with the oil and season with salt and black pepper. Spread in a single layer and roast until crisp and golden, about 15 minutes. Let cool.

Place a pizza stone in the upper third of the oven and increase the oven temperature to 475°F (245°C).

Divide the dough in half. On a lightly floured work surface, stretch half of the dough into a 12-inch (30-cm) round. Transfer the dough to a lightly floured pizza peel. Spread half of the pizza sauce evenly over the dough, leaving a 1½-inch (4-cm) border uncovered. Sprinkle half of the mozzarella on the sauce, dollop with half of the ricotta, and sprinkle with half of the dried oregano. Arrange half of the artichokes and half of the olives on top.

Using the pizza peel, transfer the pizza to the preheated pizza stone. Bake until the crust is deep golden and the cheese is bubbling, 10-12 minutes.

Using the pizza peel, transfer the pizza to a cutting board and let cool for 3 minutes. Sprinkle with red pepper flakes and garnish with oregano sprigs. Cut into slices and serve immediately. Repeat with the second half of the dough, or wrap tightly with plastic wrap and refrigerate for up to 3 days. The remaining toppings will keep covered in the refrigerator for up to 3 days.

Inspired by the pizza Belle was raised on at Fig's, her family's pizzeria, this recipe is for anyone who likes both sweet and salt. The contrast of sweet figs and salty prosciutto with the sharpness of Gorgonzola strikes an enticing balance, and the balsamic glaze drizzled over the top just before serving adds yet another layer of tangy flavor. This pizza is also undeniably gorgeous, which we love.

FIG, PROSCIUTTO, CARAMELIZED ONION, AND GORGONZOLA PIZZA

MAKES TWO 12-INCH (30-CM) PIZZAS; 4–8 SERVINGS

6 tablespoons (3 oz/90 g) unsalted butter

1 large yellow onion, thinly sliced

Kosher salt and freshly ground pepper

1 lb (450 g) pizza dough, homemade (page 205) or purchased

All-purpose flour, for dusting

6 tablespoons (4 oz/115 g) fig jam

¼ lb (115 g) Gorgonzola cheese, crumbled

6 small fresh figs, cut into slices ⅛ inch (3 mm) thick

2 oz (60 g) thinly sliced prosciutto

Balsamic glaze, for drizzling

In a frying pan over low heat, melt the butter. Add the onion and season with salt and pepper. Cook, stirring occasionally, until the onion is meltingly tender and rich brown in color, about 40 minutes. Let cool.

Meanwhile, position a rack in the upper third of the oven and place a pizza stone on the rack. Preheat the oven to 425°F (220°C).

Divide the dough in half. On a lightly floured work surface, stretch half of the dough into a 12-inch (30-cm) round. Transfer the dough to a lightly floured pizza peel. Spread half of the fig jam evenly over the dough, leaving a 1-inch (2.5-cm) border uncovered. Sprinkle with half of the cheese and top with half of the caramelized onion.

Using the pizza peel, transfer the pizza to the preheated pizza stone. Bake until the crust is firm but not crisp, about 5 minutes. Using the pizza peel, remove the pizza from the oven and top with half of the fig slices. Return to the oven and bake until the figs are slightly caramelized and the crust is crisp and golden brown, 2–3 minutes.

Using the pizza peel, transfer the pizza to a cutting board, drape half of the prosciutto over the pizza, and drizzle with balsamic glaze. Cut the pizza into slices and serve. Repeat with the second half of the dough, or wrap tightly with plastic wrap and refrigerate for up to 3 days. The remaining toppings will keep covered in the refrigerator for up to 3 days.

Autumn in California boasts crisp days, clear skies, golden sunlight, great mushroom hunting, and usually a couple of weeks of warm weather. For this pizza, Devon uses her favorite mushrooms, which she likes to forage for, and she loves cooking it outside on her grill. We've used a conventional oven here, but feel free to move outdoors if weather permits.

WILD MUSHROOM PIZZA WITH THYME AND FONTINA

MAKES TWO 12-INCH (30-CM) PIZZAS; 4–8 SERVINGS

6 tablespoons (3 oz/90 g) unsalted butter

2 shallots, diced

¾ lb (340 g) mixed wild mushrooms, such as oyster, maitake, enoki, and/or beech, stemmed and evenly chopped

4 cloves garlic, minced

Kosher salt and freshly ground pepper

6 fresh thyme sprigs

¼ cup (2 fl oz/60 ml) dry white wine

¼ cup (2 fl oz/60 ml) heavy cream

1 lb (450 g) pizza dough, homemade (page 205) or purchased

All-purpose flour, for dusting

1 cup (8 fl oz/240 ml) White Sauce (page 205)

2 cups (8 oz/225 g) shredded fontina cheese

Position a rack in the upper third of the oven and place a pizza stone on the rack. Preheat the oven to 425°F (220°C).

In a large frying pan over medium heat, melt the butter. Add the shallots and cook, stirring occasionally, until softened, about 3 minutes. Add the mushrooms and cook, stirring occasionally, until beginning to caramelize, about 5 minutes. Add the garlic and cook, stirring occasionally, until fragrant, about 1 minute. Season with salt and pepper. Reduce the heat to medium-low, add the thyme sprigs and wine, and deglaze the pan, stirring to scrape up any browned bits from the bottom. Add the cream and cook, stirring constantly, until the liquid has evaporated, about 3 minutes. Let cool. Remove and discard the thyme sprigs.

Divide the dough in half. On a lightly floured work surface, stretch half of the dough into a 12-inch (30-cm) round. Transfer the dough to a lightly floured pizza peel. Spread half of the white sauce evenly over the dough, leaving a 1-inch (2.5-cm) border uncovered. Sprinkle ½ cup (2 oz/60 g) of the cheese over the sauce. Spread half of the mushroom mixture evenly on top and sprinkle with ½ cup (2 oz/60 g) of the cheese.

Transfer the pizza to the preheated pizza stone. Bake until the crust is deep golden and the cheese is bubbling, 7–8 minutes.

Using the pizza peel, transfer the pizza to a cutting board and let cool for 3 minutes. Cut the pizza into slices and serve immediately. Repeat with the second ball of dough, or wrap tightly with plastic wrap and refrigerate for up to 3 days. The remaining toppings will keep covered in the refrigerator for up to 3 days.

This recipe is so comforting it feels like a big ol' hug. Inspired by Belle's mom's recipe, a white bean pasta served on chilly East Coast nights, this dish is quick to whip together when you are craving a cozy meal. Paccheri, which comes in both smooth and ridged versions, is a large tubular pasta popular in southern Italy, but rigatoni, penne, or ziti would work equally well.

MOM'S "COZY LIKE A HUG" CHICKPEA PASTA

MAKES 4–6 SERVINGS

3 tablespoons plus 1 cup (8 fl oz/240 ml) extra-virgin olive oil

10 cloves garlic, sliced

3 cans (each 14½ oz/410 g) chickpeas, cannellini beans, white beans, or navy beans

1 piece Parmesan cheese rind, about 3 inches (7.5 cm) square (optional)

5 fresh thyme, rosemary, or sage sprigs

Kosher salt and freshly ground pepper

2 cups (16 fl oz/475 ml) chicken stock or vegetable stock (page 203)

1 cup (4 oz/115 g) grated Parmesan cheese, plus more for serving

Finely grated zest and juice of ½ lemon

¾ lb (340 g) dried paccheri or other tubular pasta

In a large frying pan over medium-high heat, warm 3 tablespoons of the oil. Add the garlic and cook, stirring, until lightly golden and crisp, about 2 minutes. Add the chickpeas and their liquid and cook, stirring, until slightly broken down, about 3 minutes. Add the remaining 1 cup (8 fl oz/240 ml) olive oil, the Parmesan rind (if using), and the thyme sprigs. Season with salt and pepper. Reduce the heat to medium and continue to cook, stirring occasionally, until the chickpeas have softened and begun to break down, about 10 minutes. Add the chicken stock and cook, stirring occasionally, until the chickpeas are almost completely broken down, about 15 minutes longer. Stir in the grated Parmesan and lemon juice and season to taste with salt and pepper.

While the chickpeas are cooking, bring a large pot two-thirds full of salted water to a boil over high heat. Add the pasta and cook until al dente according to the package instructions. Transfer the pasta directly from the cooking water to the pan with the chickpea mixture. Add ½ cup (4 fl oz/120 ml) of the pasta water and toss to coat.

Divide the pasta among bowls, garnish with several grinds of pepper, the lemon zest, and more grated Parmesan. Serve immediately.

With two chef parents and an Italian grandmother, Thanksgiving meals at Belle's were nothing short of fantastic. Out of all the English family's menus, one course remains consistent: an appetizer consisting of, in Belle's words, "a big ol' serving of lasagna!" Belle explains, "Over time this recipe has evolved from a classic mozzarella, ricotta, and marinara to a Bolognese base, the first recipe my father ever taught me how to cook. And I swapped out the ricotta for a Parmesan béchamel, because why not? The family lasagna recipe as it stands today is a culmination of my grandmother, my dad, and me working together. There is one important step not included in the recipe: the nap you have to take between this and the rest of the meal. Don't skip this one!" For a photo, see page 220.

ENGLISH FAMILY LASAGNA

MAKES 12 SERVINGS

FOR THE BOLOGNESE SAUCE
3 tablespoons extra-virgin olive oil, plus more for assembling

¾ lb (340 g) ground veal or beef

¾ lb (340 g) ground beef chuck

¾ lb (340 g) ground pork

Kosher salt and freshly ground pepper

5 tablespoons (2½ oz/70 g) unsalted butter

1 yellow onion, diced

2 carrots, peeled and diced

6 cloves garlic, minced

2 tablespoons tomato paste

½ cup (4 fl oz/120 ml) dry red wine

2 cans (each 28 oz/800 g) whole San Marzano whole tomatoes with juices

2 cups (8 oz/225 g) grated Parmesan cheese

1½ cups (12 fl oz/350 ml) half-and-half

To make the Bolognese, in a large Dutch oven over medium-high heat, warm the olive oil. Add the veal, beef, and pork and cook, breaking up the meat into small pieces with a wooden spoon, until browned, about 10 minutes. Season with salt and pepper, then use a slotted spoon to transfer the meat to a bowl. Reduce the heat to medium, then add the butter, scraping up any browned bits from the bottom of the pan. Add the onion and carrots and cook, stirring, until tender, about 10 minutes. Add the garlic and cook, stirring occasionally, until fragrant, about 1 minute. Stir in the tomato paste until combined, then add the wine. Cook until the wine has evaporated, 3–5 minutes.

Using your hands, crush the tomatoes as you add them to the pot. Add their juices, stir to combine, increase the heat to high, bring to a boil, and boil for 5 minutes. Return the meat to the pot, then add the Parmesan and ¾ cup (6 fl oz/180 ml) of the half-and-half. Bring to a vigorous simmer, let simmer for 5–7 minutes, then stir in the remaining half-and-half. Continue to cook for a few minutes, then reduce the heat to low to maintain a gentle simmer. Cook, uncovered and stirring occasionally, until reduced, about 1 hour. Taste and adjust the seasoning with salt and pepper if necessary.

FOR THE BÉCHAMEL

7 tablespoons (3½ oz/100 g)
unsalted butter

¼ cup (1 oz/30 g) plus 3 tablespoons
all-purpose flour

6 cups (48 fl oz/1.4 l) whole milk

1½ cups (6 oz/170 g) grated
Parmesan cheese

Kosher salt and freshly ground pepper

1 lb (450 g) dried lasagna noodles

1¼ lb (570 g) fresh mozzarella cheese,
ripped into ½-inch (12-mm) pieces

½ cup (2 oz/60 g) grated
Parmesan cheese

To make the béchamel, in a large, heavy saucepan over medium heat, melt the butter. When it starts to foam, whisk in the flour until it forms a paste. Continue to cook, whisking occasionally, until the flour turns a light golden brown and begins to smell nutty, 3–4 minutes. Add the milk and whisk until combined. Increase the heat to medium-high and bring to a simmer. Simmer for 5 minutes, then reduce the heat to medium-low and cook, whisking occasionally, until the béchamel thickens and becomes smooth and velvety, 10–12 minutes. Whisk in the Parmesan and season with salt and pepper. Set aside to cool slightly.

Bring a large pot two-thirds full of heavily salted water to a boil. Drop in half of the noodles and stir to separate the noodles as much as possible. Cook until parcooked, about 4 minutes. Use tongs to transfer to a large sieve and run under cold water. Carefully separate the noodles and lay flat on a baking sheet, separating layers of noodles with a piece of parchment. Repeat with the other half of the noodles.

Preheat the oven to 325°F (165°C). Grease a 9-by-13-inch (23-by-33-cm) baking dish with oil. To assemble the lasagna, pour 1 scant cup (scant 8 fl oz/240 ml) of the Bolognese on the bottom of the dish. Arrange a third of the noodles in an even layer over the Bolognese, then top with half of the remaining Bolognese, a third of the béchamel, and half of the mozzarella. Repeat the layering of noodles, Bolognese, béchamel, and mozzarella, then top with a final layer of noodles, the remaining béchamel, and an even sprinkling of the Parmesan.

Cover the lasagna with an oiled piece of aluminum foil, oiled side down, and place on a rimmed baking sheet. Bake for 1 hour, then uncover and increase the oven temperature to 450°F (230°C). Bake until the lasagna is deep golden brown, the cheese is bubbling, and the noodles on top are crisp, about 10 minutes longer. Let rest for 15 minutes, then cut into squares and serve.

Fresh pappardelle is the traditional partner for Italian ragù, a rich pasta sauce usually made with ground meat and tomatoes. Here, we showcase a vegetable-forward ragù, which gets its hearty texture from a mix of mushrooms and its richness from Parmesan and a splash of cream. The pasta recipe calls for 00 flour, which is more finely ground and has a lower gluten content than all-purpose flour, but you can substitute 2½ cups (11 oz/310 g) all-purpose flour.

HAND-CUT PAPPARDELLE WITH MUSHROOM RAGÙ

MAKES 4-6 SERVINGS

FOR THE PAPPARDELLE
2¼ cups (9 oz/260 g) plus
1 tablespoon 00 flour

2 teaspoons kosher salt

2 large eggs plus 5 large egg yolks

1 teaspoon extra-virgin olive oil

1–2 tablespoons water

Semolina flour, for dusting

To make the pappardelle, in the bowl of a stand mixer fitted with the paddle attachment, beat together the 00 flour and salt on low speed until combined. Increase the speed to medium, add the whole eggs, egg yolks, and oil, and beat until the dough is crumbly, about 1 minute. Add 1 tablespoon of the water and continue to beat until the dough comes together in a single mass, about 3 minutes. If the dough seems dry, add the remaining 1 tablespoon water.

Dust a work surface with semolina flour. Turn the dough out onto the floured surface and press it together. Knead the dough until firm and smooth, about 10 minutes. Shape the dough into a ball, then flatten into a disk and wrap tightly in plastic wrap. Let stand at room temperature for 30 minutes.

Set up a pasta roller according to the manufacturer's instructions. Cut the dough into 4 equal pieces. Working with 1 piece of dough at a time, and keeping the other pieces covered with a kitchen towel, gently flatten the dough into a rectangle thin enough to fit through the pasta roller on the widest setting (about ¼ inch/6 mm). Alternatively, use a handheld pasta roller to flatten the pasta dough into a rectangle about ¼ inch (6 mm) thick.

With the pasta roller set to the widest setting, roll the dough through twice. Place the dough on your work surface and fold it into thirds. Adjust the roller to the second widest setting and roll again. Repeat the process, setting the pasta roller one notch narrower each time, until you can just see your hand through the dough, about setting 4, depending on the model.

FOR THE MUSHROOM RAGÙ

¼ cup (2 fl oz/60 ml) extra-virgin olive oil, plus more as needed

1 large yellow onion, diced

1 celery stalk, diced

1 carrot, peeled and diced

1 parsnip, peeled and diced

3 cloves garlic, minced

1 oz (30 g) dried porcini mushrooms, soaked in hot water for 20 minutes then drained and chopped

Kosher salt and freshly ground pepper

½ cup (4 oz/115 g) unsalted butter, cut into pieces

1 lb (450 g) assorted fresh mushrooms, such as king oyster, portobello, and trumpet, stemmed and cut into ½-inch (12-mm) pieces

¾ cup (6 fl oz/180 ml) dry red wine

1 tablespoon tomato paste

2 cans (each 28 oz/800 g) diced tomatoes with juices

1 piece Parmesan cheese rind, about 3 inches (7.5 cm) square

2 fresh rosemary sprigs

1 cup (4 oz/115 g) grated Parmesan cheese, plus more for serving

¼ cup (2 fl oz/60 ml) heavy cream

Line a baking sheet with parchment paper. Dust the rolled-out sheet of dough with semolina flour, then trim the rounded ends to form a neat rectangle; discard the scraps. Cut the dough crosswise into 3 equal pieces, each 10–12 inches (25–30 cm) long and about 5 inches (13 cm) wide, then cut each piece lengthwise into 4 strips, each about 1¼ inches (3 cm) wide. Toss with semolina flour and transfer to the prepared baking sheet. Cover loosely with a kitchen towel while you repeat the process with the remaining dough. Let the pappardelle stand, covered, for up to 1 hour while you prepare the mushroom ragù.

To make the mushroom ragù, in a large frying pan over medium heat, warm the olive oil. Add the onion, celery, carrot, and parsnip and cook, stirring occasionally, until softened, about 15 minutes. Add the garlic and cook, stirring occasionally, until fragrant, about 1 minute. If the vegetables get too dry, add more olive oil.

Reduce the heat to medium-low, add the porcini mushrooms, and cook, stirring occasionally, until the mushrooms are softened and beginning to brown, about 5 minutes. Season to taste with salt and pepper. Increase the heat to medium and add the butter and fresh mushrooms. Cook, stirring occasionally, until the butter melts and the mushrooms are softened and starting to caramelize, 7–10 minutes.

Add the wine and tomato paste, bring to a gentle simmer, and cook, stirring occasionally, until the liquid has evaporated, about 3 minutes. Add the tomatoes with their juices and stir to combine, then add the Parmesan rind and rosemary sprigs. Simmer over medium heat until the sauce is slightly reduced, about 10 minutes. Stir in ½ cup (2 oz/60 g) of the Parmesan and the cream and season to taste with salt and pepper. Reduce the heat to low and keep warm while you cook the pasta, then remove and discard the Parmesan rind and rosemary sprigs.

Bring a large pot two-thirds full of salted water to a boil over high heat. Add the pappardelle and cook until al dente, about 3 minutes.

Using a fine-mesh sieve, transfer the pappardelle directly from the cooking water to the pan with the sauce and toss to coat. Add ½ cup (4 fl oz/120 ml) of the pasta cooking water and the remaining ½ cup (2 oz/55 g) Parmesan. Toss to combine and continue cooking until the sauce is silky and coats the pasta, 2–3 minutes. Divide the pasta among bowls, top with more Parmesan, and serve.

Although pesto is traditionally made with fresh basil, almost any tender herb and such greens as spinach, arugula, baby kale, and even chard can be used. That makes this recipe a great way to use up leftover herbs and greens in the fridge that are on the verge of wilting. You can also use any nut for the pesto, and though we call for pappardelle, you can use nearly any noodle—short, long, dried, fresh—too. In other words, you can't go wrong with this recipe. Use what you've got. The result is sure to be delicious.

PAPPARDELLE WITH HERB DRAWER PESTO

MAKES 4-6 SERVINGS

2 cloves garlic

6 cups (about 6 oz/170 g) mixed lightly packed fresh herbs and greens, such as basil, parsley, tarragon, chives, arugula, spinach, baby kale, and/or chard

1 cup (4 oz/115 g) grated Parmesan cheese, plus more for serving

½ cup (2¼ oz/65 g) toasted chopped nuts, such as pine nuts, walnuts, pistachios, and/or almonds

Juice of 1 lemon

¾ cup (6 fl oz/180 ml) extra-virgin olive oil

Kosher salt and freshly ground pepper

Fresh pappardelle (page 100) or ¾ lb (340 g) dried pappardelle, fettuccine, or linguine

With a food processor running, drop the garlic cloves through the feed tube to mince them. Add the herbs and greens, Parmesan, nuts, and lemon juice to the food processor and pulse until the greens are finely chopped, about 30 seconds. With the food processor running, slowly drizzle in the olive oil, continuing to process until well combined. Season with salt and pepper and set aside.

Bring a large pot two-thirds full of salted water to a boil over high heat. Add the pasta and cook until al dente according to the package instructions. Drain the pasta in a fine-mesh sieve, reserving ½ cup (4 fl oz/125 ml) of the pasta cooking water. Return the pasta to the pot.

Place the pot over low heat, add the pesto and reserved pasta water, and toss to coat. Season with salt and pepper. Divide the pasta among warmed bowls and serve immediately, passing more Parmesan alongside.

Utterly simple yet supremely satisfying, this pasta dish is a standby at restaurants throughout Rome. Because the recipe is so elemental, it's essential to use the highest-quality ingredients you can find for the best possible results, so seek out Italian-imported Parmesan and pecorino.

CACIO E PEPE CLASSICO

MAKES 4–6 SERVINGS

1 lb (450 g) dried spaghetti

6 tablespoons (3 oz/90 g) unsalted butter

2 teaspoons freshly ground pepper

1½ cups (6 oz/170 g) grated Parmesan cheese

⅔ cup (2½ oz/70 g) grated pecorino cheese

Kosher salt

Bring a large pot two-thirds full of salted water to a boil over high heat. Add the pasta and cook until al dente according to the package instructions. Drain the pasta in a fine-mesh sieve, reserving 1 cup (8 fl oz/240 ml) of the pasta cooking water.

Return the pot to the stovetop and reduce the heat to medium. Add the butter. When the butter has melted, add the cooked pasta and toss to coat. Add the pepper, Parmesan, pecorino, and salt to taste and toss to combine, adding the reserved pasta water a little bit at a time as needed to achieve a creamy consistency.

Divide the pasta among individual bowls and serve immediately.

This is Devon's quick plant-based creamy sauce for a cozy day. It's filled with simple nutrients, so you feel good beyond the pasta moment! You can use this sauce with gluten-free or grain-free pasta or even over roasted vegetables.

PLANT-POWERED CACIO E PEPE

MAKES 2–4 SERVINGS

½ lb (225 g) dried short pasta, such as garganelli or penne

½ cup (2 oz/60 g) raw whole cashews

½ cup (3 oz/80 g) hemp seeds

1 clove garlic, or ¼ teaspoon garlic powder

¾ cup (1½ oz/45 g) nutritional yeast

1 cup (8 fl oz/240 ml) unsweetened plain plant-based milk

Juice of ½ lemon

Kosher salt and freshly ground pepper

Bring a large pot two-thirds full of salted water to a boil over high heat. Add the pasta and cook until al dente according to the package instructions.

Meanwhile, in a blender, combine the cashews, hemp seeds, garlic clove, nutritional yeast, milk, lemon juice, 1½ teaspoons salt, and ¾ teaspoon pepper. Blend on high speed until smooth and creamy, about 1 minute.

Drain the pasta in a fine-mesh sieve, reserving about ¼ cup (2 fl oz/60 ml) of the pasta water, then return the pasta to the pot. Pour the sauce over the pasta and stir to coat, adding the reserved cooking water 1 tablespoon at a time to loosen the sauce if needed. Season to taste with salt and pepper. Divide the pasta among individual bowls and serve immediately.

TIP *Be sure to use a plain plant-based milk with no additives. This recipe is very easy to scale up. Just double everything!*

This rich and creamy Roman pasta dish is traditionally made with guanciale—pork cheek that resembles unsmoked bacon and is cured with salt, pepper, and sometimes garlic. Pancetta makes a fine substitute. Although some restaurant kitchens add cream to this recipe, it isn't necessary. The combination of cheese and eggs results in a very creamy sauce.

SPAGHETTI ALLA CARBONARA

MAKES 4–6 SERVINGS

3 large eggs, at room temperature

1½ cups (6 oz/170 g) grated pecorino romano cheese, plus more for serving

2 tablespoons extra-virgin olive oil

6 oz (170 g) guanciale or pancetta, diced

Kosher salt and freshly ground pepper

1 lb (450 g) spaghetti

In a bowl, whisk together the eggs and cheese. Set aside.

In a 12-inch (30-cm) frying pan over medium heat, warm the olive oil. Add the guanciale and cook, stirring occasionally, until browned and the fat has rendered, 8–10 minutes. Set aside.

Meanwhile, bring a large pot two-thirds full of salted water to a boil over high heat. Add the pasta and cook until al dente according to the package instructions. Drain the pasta in a fine-mesh sieve, reserving 1 cup (8 fl oz/240 ml) of the pasta cooking water.

Slowly whisk ½ cup (4 fl oz/120 ml) of the pasta cooking water into the egg-cheese mixture.

Return the frying pan with the guanciale to medium heat and rewarm. Add the pasta and ¼ cup (2 fl oz/60 ml) of the reserved cooking water to the pan and toss to combine. Remove the pan from the heat, pour in the egg mixture, and toss well to combine. Season generously with pepper. Serve immediately, passing additional cheese alongside.

This dish is the epitome of Italian cooking: simple, fresh, and satisfying. We love bucatini, a thick noodle with a hollow center, because it's hearty and coats in sauce beautifully. Especially this one—a silky smooth, bright, and tangy combination of butter, a little cream, fresh lemon juice, and the not-so-secret key to the perfect pasta sauce: pasta cooking water.

BUCATINI AL LIMONE

MAKES 4-6 SERVINGS

Kosher salt

1 lb (450 g) bucatini

½ cup (4 oz/115 g) unsalted butter, cut into 4 pieces

1½ teaspoons freshly ground pepper, plus more for serving

1¼ cups (10 fl oz/300 ml) heavy cream

Finely grated zest and juice of 1 lemon

2 cups (8 oz/225 g) grated Parmesan cheese, plus more for serving

Zest of 1 lemon, removed in long strips, then cut into strips ⅛ inch (3 mm) wide, for garnish

Bring a large pot two-thirds full of salted water to a boil over high heat. Add the pasta and cook until very al dente, about 2 minutes less than in the package instructions. Drain the pasta in a fine-mesh sieve, reserving 1¼ cups (10 fl oz/300 ml) of the pasta cooking water. Set aside.

Meanwhile, make the sauce. In a large pot over medium heat, melt the butter. Add the pepper and cook, stirring frequently, until toasted, about 2 minutes. Slowly pour in the cream, whisking constantly, until the sauce is emulsified and begins to simmer, about 2 minutes. Add the finely grated lemon zest and a generous pinch of salt, stirring to combine.

Increase the heat to medium-high. Transfer the bucatini to the sauce, then add ¾ cup (6 fl oz/180 ml) of the pasta water. Slowly add the Parmesan to the sauce, tossing the pasta constantly, until creamy and smooth. Stir in the lemon juice. If desired, add more of the pasta water by the tablespoon to loosen the sauce a bit (up to ½ cup/4 fl oz/120 ml). Season to taste with salt.

Divide the pasta among warmed bowls, garnish with the lemon zest strips, more Parmesan, and a few grinds of pepper, and serve immediately.

This pasta dish was inspired by an unforgettable meal that Belle ate in the small town of Usini, Sardinia. It gets a double dose of simple but flavorful sauces: first, it's tossed with a tomato-based sauce, then it's drizzled with fresh basil pesto (or a "pesto floater," as we call it in the Test Kitchen). The recipe calls for a rustic cut of pasta called strozzapreti, which has an elongated, twisted shape that pairs well with hearty sauces. Then it's finished with pecorino sardo, a lightly salty, mildly tangy Sardinian cheese made with milk from the island's sheep. If you can't find either, substitute your favorite short noodle pasta and pecorino romano cheese.

STROZZAPRETI POMODORO WITH PESTO AND PECORINO SARDO

MAKES 4-6 SERVINGS

1½ cups (12 fl oz/350 ml) Belle's Pomodoro Sauce (page 204) or your favorite tomato-based pasta sauce

Kosher salt

1 lb (450 g) strozzapreti

¾ cup (3 oz/90 g) grated Parmesan cheese

1 cup (8½ oz/240 g) basil pesto, homemade (page 212) or purchased

Grated pecorino sardo cheese, for serving

Fresh basil leaves, for garnish

Warm the pomodoro sauce in a large saucepan over medium-low heat.

Bring a large pot two-thirds full of salted water to a boil over high heat. Add the pasta and cook until al dente according to the package instructions. Using a fine-mesh sieve, transfer the pasta directly from the cooking water to the pan with the pomodoro sauce. Sprinkle with the Parmesan and toss to coat. For a thinner sauce, add ¼–½ cup (2–4 fl oz/60–120 ml) of the pasta water and stir until silky and emulsified.

Transfer the pasta and sauce to a wide serving bowl and drizzle with the pesto. Sprinkle with the pecorino sardo, garnish with basil leaves, and serve immediately.

Is there anything better than a warm bowl of saucy noodles? The answer, in our Test Kitchen, is a firm no! This recipe was inspired by the iconic dish at Carbone, a staple New York eatery, and is the perfect balance of sweet tomato and spicy Calabrian chile. We suggest using mezzi rigatoni, a slightly smaller, curved version of the classic pasta shape, as it provides better pockets for trapping the wonderfully flavorful yet wildly simple sauce.

NEW YORK, NY, SPICY RIGATONI

MAKES 4–6 SERVINGS

3 tablespoons extra-virgin olive oil

2 shallots, finely chopped

3 cloves garlic, minced

Kosher salt and freshly ground pepper

⅔ cup (6 oz/170 g) tomato paste

2 tablespoons crushed Calabrian chile

4 tablespoons (2 oz/60 g) unsalted butter, cut into 4 pieces

¼ cup (2 fl oz/60 ml) vodka

1½ cups (12 fl oz/350 ml) heavy cream

1 lb (450 g) mezzi rigatoni or other short pasta

1½ cups (6 oz/170 g) grated Parmesan cheese, plus more for serving

In a large, deep frying pan over medium heat, warm the oil. Add the shallots and cook, stirring, until softened, 4–5 minutes. Add the garlic and cook until lightly toasted and fragrant, about 1 minute. Season with a pinch of salt. Add the tomato paste and Calabrian chile, stir to combine, and then cook, stirring occasionally, until the tomato paste is toasted and turns dark red, about 6 minutes; watch carefully so the mixture does not burn. Add the butter and cook, stirring, until the sauce comes together, about 13 minutes. Add the vodka and stir, scraping up any browned bits at the bottom of the pan, until mostly absorbed, about 30 seconds. Reduce the heat to low and add the cream. Stir until well combined, and gently simmer while you make the pasta.

Bring a large pot two-thirds full of salted water to a boil over high heat. Add the pasta and cook until al dente according to the package instructions.

Increase the heat for the sauce to medium-low, then, using a fine-mesh sieve, transfer the pasta directly to the sauce. Add the Parmesan and 1 cup (8 fl oz/240 ml) of the pasta water and cook, stirring and tossing the pasta, until the cheese has emulsified into the sauce and the sauce looks smooth and silky, about 3 minutes. The pasta should be very saucy.

Adjust the seasoning with salt and pepper. Divide the pasta among warmed bowls, garnish with more Parmesan and pepper, and serve.

TIP Calabrian chiles come in different forms: fresh, dried, chopped, sliced, crushed, whole, and even as a paste. For the best results, we recommend using jarred crushed Calabrian chiles, but chopped will work as well.

If you are looking for a simple, comforting bowl of spaghetti with a slight twist, you are in the right place! We love substituting turkey for traditional beef, as turkey is leaner and gives the dish a different, lighter vibe. Adding onion and carrot for some natural sweetness pairs perfectly with the earthy, slightly peppery flavor of sage. This is one of our favorites—and that's saying a lot since we have a ton of recipes for spaghetti and meatballs.

SPAGHETTI AND TURKEY MEATBALLS

MAKES 4–6 SERVINGS

3 tablespoons plus ¼ cup (2 fl oz/60 ml) extra-virgin olive oil

½ yellow onion, grated

½ large carrot, grated

Kosher salt and freshly ground pepper

1 lb (450 g) ground turkey, dark and light meat

1½ cups (2¼ oz/65 g) fine fresh bread crumbs

1 large egg, whisked

2 teaspoons finely chopped fresh sage

2 cans (each 28 oz/800 g) whole plum tomatoes, preferably San Marzano, with juices

2 cloves garlic, minced

1 teaspoon dried oregano

1 lb (450 g) spaghetti

Grated Parmesan cheese, for serving

In a large frying pan over medium-high heat, warm 1 tablespoon of the oil. Add the onion, carrot, and a few pinches of salt and cook, stirring, until soft, about 5 minutes. Transfer to a large bowl and let cool.

Add the ground turkey, bread crumbs, egg, sage, 1 teaspoon salt, and ½ teaspoon pepper. Mix gently but thoroughly with your hands. Scoop up about 3 tablespoons of the mixture and form into a meatball. Repeat to make 12 meatballs total.

In the frying pan over medium-high heat, warm 2 tablespoons of the oil. Add the meatballs and cook, turning, until browned on all sides, about 5 minutes. Transfer to a plate.

Add the tomatoes with their juices to a food processor. While pulsing, slowly stream the remaining ¼ cup (2 fl oz/60 ml) olive oil through the feed tube until the tomatoes are pureed but still a bit chunky. Stir in the garlic and oregano and season with salt and pepper.

Pour the tomato sauce into the frying pan over medium heat. Add the meatballs, cover, and reduce the heat to low. Simmer, stirring occasionally, until the meatballs are cooked through, about 30 minutes.

While the meatballs are cooking, bring a large pot two-thirds full of salted water to a boil over high heat. Add the pasta and cook until al dente according to the package instructions. Drain the pasta in a fine-mesh sieve, then add the pasta to the pan with the meatballs. Using tongs, gently toss to combine.

Divide the spaghetti, meatballs, and sauce among bowls. Sprinkle with Parmesan and serve immediately.

What we love about this recipe is that it is as equally as comforting (as meatballs should be) as it is fresh (thanks to all the fresh herbs and pickled onions). This Greek-inspired dish includes ground chicken, warming spices, and whole-milk yogurt, which lends moisture. To complete this soul-satisfying meal, the meatballs are baked atop a bed of orzo tossed with kale, tangy feta cheese, and a trio of herbs. A garnish of quick-pickled red onion adds a pop of brightness and crunch. The same pot is used for cooking both the meatballs and the orzo, making cleanup a breeze.

GREEK CHICKEN MEATBALLS WITH ORZO AND FETA

MAKES 4-6 SERVINGS

FOR THE MEATBALLS

3 tablespoons extra-virgin olive oil

1 large yellow onion, finely diced

4 cloves garlic, minced

1½ tablespoons dried oregano

1 tablespoon ground cumin

2 teaspoons ground coriander

1 teaspoon red pepper flakes (optional)

¾ lb (340 g) ground chicken breast meat

¾ lb (340 g) ground chicken thigh meat

1 large egg

½ cup (1¾ oz/50 g) panko bread crumbs

¼ cup (2 oz/60 g) plus 2 tablespoons plain whole-milk Greek yogurt

2 teaspoons finely grated lemon zest

Kosher salt and freshly ground black pepper

¼ cup (2 fl oz/60 ml) neutral oil, such as canola, plus more as needed

To make the meatballs, in a Dutch oven over medium heat, warm the olive oil. Add the onion and cook, stirring occasionally, until softened, about 8 minutes. Add the garlic and cook, stirring occasionally, until fragrant, about 1 minute. Add the oregano, cumin, coriander, and red pepper flakes (if using) and stir until the onion is evenly coated, about 30 seconds. Remove from the heat and let cool completely.

In a large bowl, combine the ground chicken, the cooled onion mixture, the egg, panko, yogurt, lemon zest, 2 tablespoons salt, and 2 teaspoons black pepper. Using your hands, gently but thoroughly mix until combined. Using a large spoon, form the meat mixture into 16–18 meatballs, each about 1½ inches (4 cm) in diameter.

Wipe out the pot used to cook the onion, set over medium-high heat, and warm the neutral oil. Working in batches, add the meatballs and sear, turning occasionally, until well browned all over, about 6 minutes per batch. Transfer to a plate. Add more oil to the pot between batches as needed. Wipe out the pot.

Preheat the oven to 425°F (220°C).

Continues on next page

Continued from previous page

FOR THE ORZO

5 tablespoons (2½ oz/70 g) unsalted butter

3 cloves garlic, minced

1 lb (450 g) orzo pasta

¼ cup (2 fl oz/60 ml) dry white wine

4 cups (32 fl oz/950 ml) chicken stock, homemade (page 203) or purchased

Kosher salt and freshly ground black pepper

¼ lb (115 g) baby kale, coarsely chopped

¼ lb (115 g) feta cheese, crumbled, plus more for garnish

1½ tablespoons sherry vinegar

1 tablespoon chopped fresh mint, plus more for garnish

1 tablespoon chopped fresh dill, plus more for garnish

1 tablespoon chopped fresh oregano, plus more for garnish

Extra-virgin olive oil, for drizzling

Pickled Red Onion (page 209), for garnish

To make the orzo, in the same pot over medium heat, melt 3 tablespoons of the butter. Add the garlic and cook, stirring occasionally, until fragrant, about 1 minute. Increase the heat to medium-high, add the orzo, and stir until the orzo is coated with the butter-garlic mixture, about 30 seconds. Add the wine and stir until absorbed. Remove from the heat. Add the stock and a big pinch of salt, stirring to coat the orzo.

Cover the pot, transfer to the oven, and cook, stirring halfway through, until the orzo is just tender and the broth is absorbed, 20–25 minutes.

Remove the pot from the oven. Stir in the remaining 2 tablespoons butter, the kale, feta, vinegar, mint, dill, and oregano, stirring until the butter is melted and the kale is wilted. Season to taste with salt and black pepper.

Arrange the meatballs on top, nesting them slightly in the orzo. Drizzle olive oil over all. Return the pot, uncovered, to the oven and cook until the meatballs are cooked through, about 5 minutes.

Garnish with feta, mint, dill, oregano, and pickled onion and serve immediately.

One of the best dishes to master is classic risotto. It's simple, easy to personalize, and always a crowd-pleaser. We call for Arborio rice, a short, starchy Italian variety that provides the perfect consistency, unless you overcook it—the most common risotto woe. To avoid a soggy result, be sure to slowly add the stock and, as always, taste as you go. You're looking for a smooth, creamy consistency that still has bite and texture.

CLASSIC PARMESAN RISOTTO

MAKES 6-8 SERVINGS

2 qt (1.9 l) chicken stock, homemade (page 203) or purchased

2 tablespoons extra-virgin olive oil

2 shallots, finely diced

3 cloves garlic, minced

Kosher salt and freshly ground pepper

2 cups (14 oz/400 g) Arborio rice

½ cup (4 fl oz/120 ml) dry white wine

1 cup (4 oz/115 g) grated Parmesan cheese, plus shaved for serving

4 tablespoons (2 oz/60 g) unsalted butter, cut into 4 pieces

½ cup (4 fl oz/120 ml) heavy cream

Juice of ½ lemon

In a saucepan over medium-high heat, bring the stock to a simmer. Reduce the heat to low and keep the stock warm.

In a large pot over medium heat, warm the oil. Add the shallots and cook, stirring, until softened, about 3 minutes. Add the garlic and cook, stirring occasionally, until fragrant, about 1 minute. Season with salt and pepper. Add the rice and cook, stirring, until the grains are slightly translucent, about 1 minute, then add the wine and cook, stirring occasionally, until the liquid is absorbed, about 2 minutes.

Begin adding the warm stock 1 cup (8 fl oz/240 ml) at a time, stirring frequently after each addition. Wait until the stock is almost completely absorbed before adding more. When the rice is tender yet still slightly firm to the bite, after about 20 minutes, add the Parmesan, butter, and cream and cook, stirring, until the risotto is creamy and smooth, about 2 minutes. Stir in the lemon juice and season with salt and pepper.

Divide the risotto among warmed bowls. Garnish with Parmesan shavings and a few grinds of pepper and serve immediately.

For this savory galette, we borrowed flavors from classic French onion soup: caramelized onions, beef broth, dry sherry, and nutty Gruyère cheese. When cooking the onions on the stovetop, don't rush the process. Sizzling them slowly allows the natural sugars to caramelize, yielding richly browned onions that are wonderfully sweet. Cut the galette into small slices and serve as an elegant appetizer or enjoy as a side dish with Belle's pan-seared ribeye steaks (page 150).

FRENCH ONION GALETTE

MAKES 6-8 SERVINGS

FOR THE CARAMELIZED ONION
2 tablespoons unsalted butter

1 large yellow onion, halved through the stem end, then halves cut lengthwise into wedges 1 inch (2.5 cm) wide, keeping root end intact

Pinch of sugar

Kosher salt and freshly ground pepper

¼ cup (2 fl oz/60 ml) dry sherry

½ cup (4 fl oz/120 ml) beef broth or vegetable stock (page 203)

4 fresh thyme sprigs

FOR THE GALETTE
All-purpose flour, for dusting

1 sheet (14 oz/400 g) frozen puff pastry, thawed

2 tablespoons Dijon mustard

1 cup (4 oz/115 g) grated Gruyère cheese

1 large egg, beaten with 1 tablespoon water

Kosher salt and freshly ground pepper

Chopped fresh chives, for garnish

Fresh thyme leaves, for garnish

To make the caramelized onion, in a large frying pan over medium heat, melt the butter. Add the onion and cook, without stirring, until the wedges start to brown and stick to the pan, about 3 minutes. Sprinkle with the sugar and season with salt and pepper. Add the sherry and cook until almost evaporated, about 1 minute, then stir the onion, scraping up the caramelized brown bits. Cook, without stirring, until the onion is nicely browned, about 3 minutes, then add about 2 tablespoons of the broth, stirring and scraping up the caramelized brown bits. Cook, without stirring, until the onion starts to brown again, about 3 minutes, then add about 2 tablespoons of the broth, stirring and scraping up the caramelized brown bits. Repeat the process until you've used up all of the broth. Remove from the heat and stir in the thyme sprigs. Let cool.

To make the galette, line a baking sheet with parchment paper. On a lightly floured surface, roll out the puff pastry into a 14-inch (35-cm) round. Transfer to the prepared baking sheet. Brush with the mustard, leaving a 2-inch (5-cm) border uncovered, then sprinkle the cheese over the mustard. Arrange the onion wedges on top. Fold the dough up and over the filling, forming loose pleats all around the edge and leaving the center open. Lightly brush the pleated dough with the egg mixture and sprinkle with salt. Refrigerate the galette for 15-20 minutes. Meanwhile, preheat the oven to 375°F (190°C).

Bake until the crust is deep golden brown and the onion is deeply caramelized, 40–45 minutes. Transfer the baking sheet to a wire rack and let cool for 10 minutes. Garnish the galette with chives, thyme leaves, and a few grinds of pepper. Cut into slices and serve.

In the Test Kitchen, we're self-described dunkers. As soon as this bread comes out of the oven, we're pulling off chunks and dipping them into a bowl of warm marinara sauce. The heavenly combo of Parmesan cheese, fresh herbs, and marinara is reminiscent of a pizza, but this is way more fun to eat. You can make the dough yourself or purchase it from the grocery store or your favorite pizzeria. Be sure to use a small Bundt pan with a 6-cup (48-fl oz/1.4-l) capacity, not a standard-size pan.

ROSEMARY-GARLIC PULL-APART BREAD

MAKES 6 SERVINGS

6 tablespoons (3 oz/90 g) unsalted butter, melted

3 cloves garlic, minced

1 cup (4 oz/115 g) packed grated Parmesan cheese

2 tablespoons minced fresh rosemary

1 tablespoon minced fresh flat-leaf parsley

½ teaspoon kosher salt

¼ teaspoon freshly ground pepper

All-purpose flour, for dusting

2 lb (1 kg) pizza dough, homemade (page 205) or purchased, at room temperature

Flake salt

Belle's Pomodoro Sauce (page 204) or your favorite marinara sauce, warmed, for dipping (optional)

Preheat the oven to 350°F (180°C). Butter a 6-cup (48-fl oz/1.4-l) Bundt pan.

In a bowl, stir together the melted butter and garlic. In another bowl, stir together the Parmesan, rosemary, parsley, kosher salt, and pepper.

On a lightly floured work surface, cut the pizza dough into 32 pieces, each about 1 oz (30 g). Roll into balls. Working with 1 dough ball at a time, roll it in the garlic butter and then in the Parmesan mixture. Place in the prepared Bundt pan. Repeat with the remaining dough balls, arranging them side by side and then stacking them on top of one another. Butter a sheet of aluminum foil and loosely cover the pan, buttered side down.

Bake until the dough balls are puffed up above the pan rim and deeply golden, about 45 minutes, removing the foil halfway through baking. Transfer the pan to a wire rack and let cool for 10 minutes, then carefully invert the bread onto a baking sheet. Return to the oven and bake until the top is golden brown, about 15 minutes more.

Sprinkle the hot bread with flake salt and let cool for 10 minutes, then serve warm. If desired, accompany with the marinara sauce for dipping.

Continued from previous page

FOR THE BREAD

627 g (22 oz) bread flour,
plus more for dusting

36 g (1¼ oz) all-purpose flour

36 g (1¼ oz) rye flour

524 g warm filtered water
(90°–110°F/32°–43°C)

14 g (½ oz) fine sea salt

140 g (5 oz) leaven (mature
sourdough starter)

115 g (4 oz) pitted black
and green olives, finely chopped

MAKE THE BREAD

Step 1: Dough hydration In a large bowl, whisk together the flours. Pour in 514 g of the water and mix together with a rubber spatula until no dry bits remain. The dough will look ragged. Cover loosely with a kitchen towel and let stand at room temperature for 1 hour.

Step 2: Mix the dough Using your hands, gently pinch in the salt, leaven, and remaining 10 g water until combined. Pull the bottom of the dough out from underneath and fold it over on top of itself. Transfer to a large clean bowl. Re-cover with the towel and set in a warm spot (75°–80°F/24°–27°C). Let rest for 30 minutes.

Step 3: Folds and bulk fermentation Lightly dip your hand in water and pull one underside quadrant of the dough up and over the top of the dough. Repeat for each quadrant. (This builds gluten.) Re-cover and let rest in the warm spot for 30 minutes. Repeat this process every 30 minutes 4–6 more times (2–3 hours total), until the dough looks 30–50 percent larger in volume and jiggles, domes slightly, and air bubbles are visible. After the second fold, gently mix in the olives, pinching and then gently kneading them into the dough.

Step 4: Bench pre-shape and rest Gently transfer the dough to a work surface and dust it lightly with bread flour. Using a bench scraper, gently flip the dough flour side down. Lightly dip your hand in water and pull one underside quadrant up and over the top of the dough, sealing it in the middle of the top. Repeat with the remaining quadrants. Flip the dough seam side down and cover with the towel. Let rest at room temperature for 30 minutes. While the bread rests, generously flour a small (8-inch/20-cm) round bread basket with bread flour or line a medium bowl with a kitchen towel and flour the towel.

Step 5: Final shaping Dust the dough with bread flour again. Using the bench scraper, flip the dough flour side down. Dip your hand in water, then bring up each quadrant and seal on top as in step 4. Flip the dough seam side down. Using your hands and using the work surface as an anchor, pull the dough toward you to create a tightly rounded shape. Shift the dough and pull it toward you again. This motion helps mold the dough into a smooth, tight round.

Step 6: Final proof Using the bench scraper, gently flip the dough round seam side up and transfer, seam side up, to the floured bread basket. Cover with the towel and let rest in the same warm spot (75°-80°F/24°-27°C) for 2-4 hours. If it's colder, it will be 5-6 hours; if warmer, 2-3 hours. Alternatively, to develop more flavor, wrap the dough in plastic wrap (to prevent condensation) and refrigerate in the basket or bowl for 10-12 hours; bring to room temperature before baking. To check if the dough is ready to bake, gently press it with a finger; it should spring back slowly and leave a small depression. If it springs back quickly, give it more time.

Step 7: Score and bake About 30 minutes before the dough is ready, place a lidded Dutch oven in a cold oven and preheat the oven to 500°F (260°C). When the oven and dough are ready, dust the exposed side of the dough with bread flour. Line a cutting board with parchment paper and invert it over the basket. Flip the bread over onto the parchment.

Working carefully but quickly, remove the Dutch oven from the oven and remove the lid. Grab the corners of the parchment and transfer the dough, still on the parchment, to the pot. Using a sharp knife or scoring blade, score the top of the bread with an X or with a / (slash) with a slight curve. Remove the lid and return the pot to the oven. Reduce the oven temperature to 450°F (230°C) and bake for 20 minutes. Uncover and bake until the bread is dark golden, 20-25 minutes longer. To test for doneness, insert an instant-read thermometer into the center of the loaf; it should register 190°F (88°C). Transfer the bread to a wire rack and test again by lightly tapping the bottom; it should sound hollow. Let cool on a wire rack for at least 1 hour before serving.

MEAT & FISH

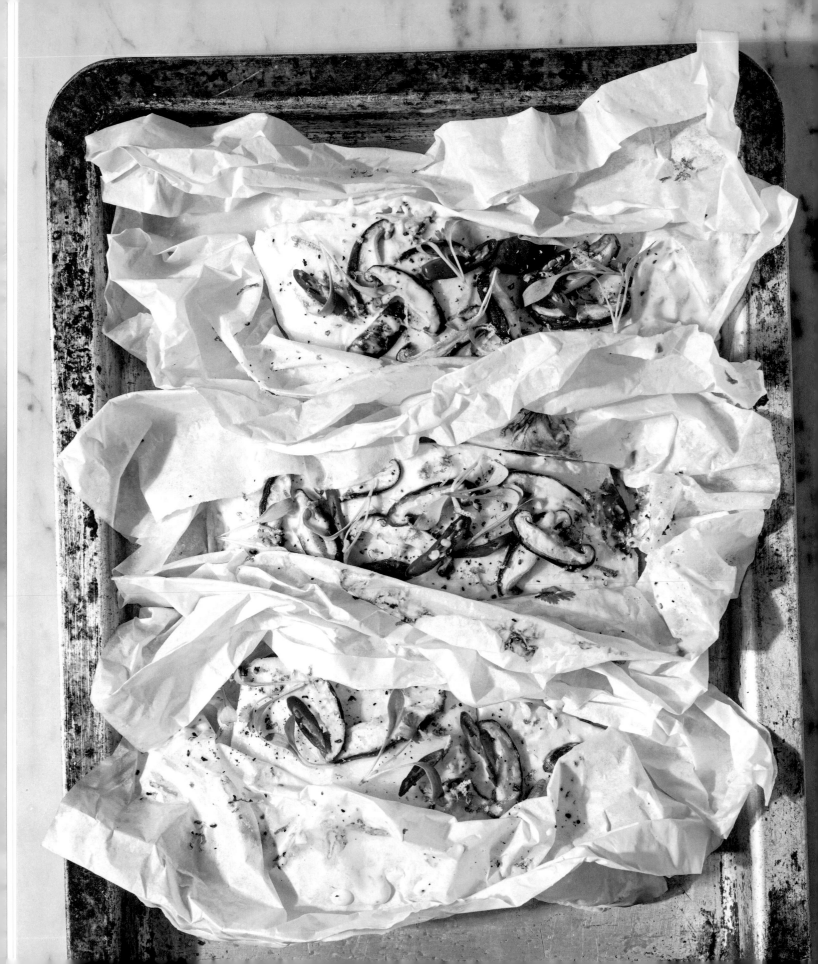

Fish en papillote is a French method of steaming fish in parchment paper, usually with herbs and aromatics, butter, vegetables, and a lemon wedge. For our version, we took inspiration from the Thai pantry, mixing together coconut milk, lemongrass, fish sauce, and lime juice, which we use to season both the fish and fresh shiitake mushrooms.

FISH EN PAPILLOTE WITH COCONUT MILK, LEMONGRASS, AND SHIITAKES

MAKES 4 SERVINGS

4 skinless flaky white fish fillets, such as cod or halibut (4–6 oz/115–170 g each)

Kosher salt and freshly ground pepper

1 cup (8 fl oz/240 ml) unsweetened coconut milk

2 teaspoons minced fresh lemongrass, tender part only

Finely grated zest and juice of 1 lime, plus 1 lime, cut into wedges

1 tablespoon fish sauce

1 tablespoon plus 1 teaspoon firmly packed coconut sugar or light brown sugar

1 clove garlic, minced

3 oz (90 g) fresh shiitake mushrooms, stems removed and caps thinly sliced (about 6 medium)

2 tablespoons fresh micro cilantro or cilantro leaves, for garnish

Thin fresh red chile slices (optional)

2 cups (11 oz/310 g) cooked white or brown rice, for serving

Preheat the oven to 350°F (180°C). Pat the fish fillets dry and season lightly with salt and pepper.

In a medium bowl, whisk together the coconut milk, lemongrass, 2 teaspoons lime juice, the fish sauce, sugar, garlic, and ½ teaspoon salt.

Cut 4 pieces of parchment paper, each about 12 by 16 inches (30 by 40 cm). Place 1 piece of parchment on a work surface with a long side facing you. Add 2 teaspoons of the coconut mixture to the center of the parchment and lay 1 fillet horizontally directly on top of the mixture. Sprinkle one-fourth of the mushrooms around and on top of the fish. Repeat with the remaining fish fillets.

To create the parchment packet, fold the long side of parchment closest to you in toward the fish so the edge just touches where the fish begins. Then fold the flap in half back toward you to create two creases. Do the same with the other long side. Once both sides are folded, bring them together to meet in the center on top of the fish. Neatly overlap the creases of the folds over each other so they match up and become one piece. Then flatten the fold by folding it away from you and under. Fold one of the open sides in half twice, then tuck it once more under the fish to seal. Pour a scant ¼ cup (2 fl oz/60 ml) of the coconut mixture into the end, then fold the end in half twice to seal (like you did for the other side). Repeat with the remaining packets.

Place the packets on a baking sheet with the ends tucked under the fish and the folded seal facing up. Bake until the fish is opaque throughout (open a packet to check), 15–18 minutes. Carefully open the packets and top with a squeeze of lime and a sprinkle of lime zest, cilantro, and chile (if using). Serve at once with the rice.

Chicken pot pie is an American classic, and to us, a nostalgic representation of the ultimate comfort food. Traditionally, it is composed of a filling of chicken, celery, carrot, and onion baked in butter-based pie pastry. In our modern version, we add mushrooms and thyme and bake the filling topped with layers of flaky phyllo dough for added savor and sophistication. Serve accompanied by a lightly dressed chicory salad and a good Sauvignon Blanc.

CHICKEN POT PIE WITH MUSHROOMS AND THYME

MAKES 8 SERVINGS

FOR THE FILLING
14 tablespoons (7 oz/200 g) unsalted butter

1 cup (4¼ oz/120 g) plus 2 tablespoons all-purpose flour

⅓ cup (2¾ fl oz/80 ml) Madeira

2 tablespoons chicken demi-glace

7 cups (56 fl oz/1.7 l) chicken stock, homemade (page 203) or purchased

1 large yellow onion, diced

4 celery stalks, sliced ⅛ inch (3 mm) thick

1 lb (450 g) cremini mushrooms, trimmed and thinly sliced

1 tablespoon chopped fresh thyme

2 teaspoons chopped fresh tarragon

1 bay leaf

½ lb (225 g) small red-skinned potatoes, cut into ½-inch (12-mm) dice

8 cups (3 lb/1.4 kg) cubed cooked chicken

1 bag (1 lb/450 g) frozen pearl onions

Fine sea salt and freshly ground pepper

To make the filling, in a 5-qt (4.7-l) Dutch oven over medium heat, melt the butter. Add the flour and cook, stirring constantly, until the mixture smells fragrant and nutty, about 2 minutes. Whisk in the Madeira and demi-glace. Slowly add the chicken stock, whisking until smooth, then bring to a boil. Add the onion, celery, mushrooms, thyme, tarragon, and bay leaf and cook until the vegetables are almost tender, about 10 minutes. Add the potatoes, chicken, and pearl onions and season with salt and pepper. Cook, stirring occasionally, until the potatoes are tender, about 10 minutes. Remove from the heat and let cool for 10 minutes, then remove the bay leaf and discard.

While the filling cools, preheat the oven to 400°F (200°C). Line a baking sheet with parchment paper.

To assemble the pot pie, on a dry work surface, gently unroll the phyllo. Cut the phyllo in half horizontally. Cover half of the phyllo with a slightly damp paper towel and set aside.

Spread 1 phyllo sheet on the work surface and, using a pastry brush, lightly brush with melted butter. Cover with a second sheet, rotating it clockwise slightly, and brush it with more butter. Repeat with the remaining sheets from one stack, rotating each one slightly and brushing each with butter. Carefully lift the stack of buttered phyllo and place it on top of the chicken mixture in the pot, folding the dough up as necessary along the edges of the pot. Brush the phyllo with the egg wash and sprinkle with salt.

FOR ASSEMBLING

1 lb (450 g) phyllo dough sheets, thawed if frozen (see Tip)

½ cup (4 oz/115 g) unsalted butter, melted

1 large egg beaten with 1 teaspoon water

Fine sea salt

Bake until the phyllo is crisp and browned all over, 15–20 minutes, covering the edges with aluminum foil about halfway through the cooking time if necessary to keep them from turning too brown. Remove from the oven and let cool for 10 minutes.

While the pot pie is cooking, prepare the remaining phyllo. Spread 1 of the remaining phyllo sheets on your work surface and, using the pastry brush, lightly brush with melted butter. Cover with a second sheet and brush it with butter. Repeat with the remaining sheets of phyllo, brushing each with butter. Using a sharp knife, cut the stack of phyllo into 8 triangles of equal size. Transfer the triangles to the prepared baking sheet.

While the pot pie is cooling, place the phyllo triangles in the oven and bake until lightly browned and crispy, 8–10 minutes.

To serve, spoon the pot pie onto warmed plates or into shallow bowls and arrange a phyllo triangle on top of each serving.

TIP **Use phyllo sheets that are larger than the circumference of the Dutch oven.**

Here are the three keys to a great roast chicken: bring the chicken to room temperature before roasting so it cooks more evenly, baste it with butter to crisp and brown the skin, and start the bird breast side down to protect it from direct heat while the legs, which require more cooking, get a head start.

THE ULTIMATE ROAST CHICKEN

MAKES 4–6 SERVINGS

1 whole chicken (about 5 lb/2.3 kg), giblets removed

1 lb (450 g) baby yellow potatoes, halved if larger than 1½ inches (4 cm) in diameter

½ lb (225 g) carrots, unpeeled, cut into 1-inch (2.5-cm) pieces

1 large yellow onion, chopped

2 whole heads garlic, tops cut off

6 fresh rosemary sprigs

6 fresh thyme sprigs

½ cup (4 fl oz/120 ml) extra-virgin olive oil

Kosher salt and freshly ground pepper

4 tablespoons (2 oz/60 g) unsalted butter, at room temperature

Flake salt

Crusty baguette, for dipping

Bring the chicken to room temperature 1 hour prior to cooking.

Preheat the oven to 425°F (220°C).

In a 12-inch (30-cm) cast-iron frying pan, combine the potatoes, carrots, onion, garlic, 3 of the rosemary sprigs, and 3 of the thyme sprigs. Pour the oil over the vegetables and toss to coat, making sure the garlic heads are placed cut side up. Season generously with kosher salt and pepper. Set aside.

Pat the chicken dry with paper towels. Season the chicken generously with kosher salt, including the cavity. Rub the butter all over the entire chicken, then truss the legs with kitchen twine and tuck the wings under the breasts to avoid burning.

Place the chicken, breast side down, on top of the vegetables. Season with a little more kosher salt and a few grinds of pepper.

Roast until the skin is browned, 25–30 minutes.

Remove from the oven and carefully flip the chicken over, breast side up. Continue to roast until the internal temperature of the breasts registers 165°F (74°C), basting the chicken and vegetables (especially the cut side of the garlic) with the accumulated juices every 10 minutes or so, 45–50 minutes longer.

Remove the chicken from the oven and allow it to rest for 10 minutes. Cut the twine to release the legs, then carve the chicken as desired. Sprinkle with flake salt, garnish with the remaining herb sprigs, and serve with a baguette for dipping into the juices.

Panzanella, a bread salad with Tuscan and Umbrian roots, traditionally combines bread, onions, summer tomatoes, and sometimes cucumbers, all dressed with a vinaigrette that includes the sweet juices of the tomatoes. Here, the addition of roast chicken turns this usual side dish into a main.

ROAST CHICKEN PANZANELLA

MAKES 4-6 SERVINGS

1 lb (950 g) sourdough bread, torn into 2-inch (5-cm) pieces

Extra-virgin olive oil

Kosher salt and freshly ground pepper

1 whole chicken (4-5 lb/1.8-2.3 kg), cut into 8 pieces

2½ lb (1.1 kg) assorted heirloom tomatoes, cored, seeded, and roughly chopped

½ cup (2¼ oz/65 g) pine nuts

1 small shallot, minced

2 cloves garlic, minced

2 teaspoons white wine vinegar

½ teaspoon Dijon mustard

4 tablespoons (2 oz/60 g) unsalted butter, cut into 4 pieces

1 cup (6 oz/170 g) cherry tomatoes, halved

½ cup (½ oz/15 g) fresh basil leaves, torn into small pieces, plus whole leaves for garnish

Preheat the oven to 350°F (180°C). Arrange the sourdough pieces in a single layer on a rimmed baking sheet. Drizzle with 3 tablespoons oil and season with salt and pepper. Bake until golden brown, turning once or twice, about 15 minutes. Set aside to cool completely. Increase the oven temperature to 450°F (230°C).

Arrange the chicken pieces on a rimmed baking sheet. Rub the chicken generously with oil and season with salt and pepper. Bake until the chicken is cooked through and the skin is golden brown and crispy, 40-45 minutes, or until the internal temperature of a breast is 165°F (74°C). For extra-crispy skin, turn the oven setting to broil and broil the chicken in the upper third of the oven for about 3 minutes.

While the chicken roasts, make the panzanella. In a fine-mesh sieve set over a large bowl, combine the heirloom tomatoes with 2 teaspoons salt. Set aside for 15 minutes, stirring occasionally, to allow the juices to release and drain into the bowl.

In a small frying pan over medium heat, warm 2 tablespoons oil. Add the pine nuts and cook, stirring occasionally, until toasted, about 5 minutes. Set aside.

Transfer the sieve with the tomatoes to the sink. To the tomato juices in the bowl, add the shallot, garlic, vinegar, and mustard.

Transfer the chicken to a plate. Add the butter to the baking sheet with the pan drippings and return to the oven until the butter is melted, about 1 minute. Add the pan drippings and butter to the tomato juice mixture and whisk well. Fold the toasted bread, reserved heirloom tomatoes, cherry tomatoes, torn basil, and toasted pine nuts and stir to combine. Season to taste with salt and pepper. Set aside for 5 minutes or until the bread has absorbed the liquid. Transfer to a serving platter, top with the chicken pieces, and garnish with a few grinds of pepper and basil leaves.

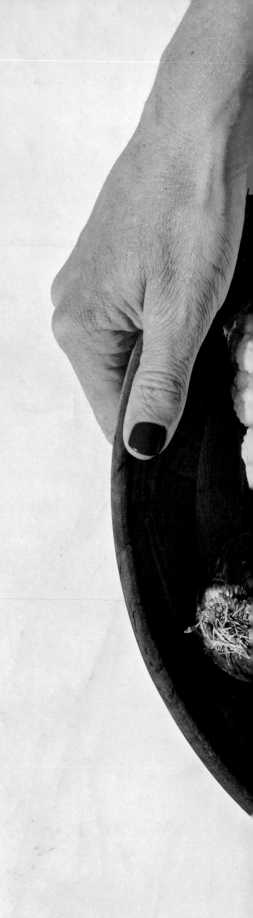

VEGETABLES

We love a good plant-based burger. Here, the mushrooms, smoked paprika, and Worcestershire (or vegan coconut aminos) create the meaty texture and umami-rich flavors of a classic burger. Tuck it inside a bun and top with your favorite fixings, or serve it wrapped in a lettuce leaf or over a green salad. If you prefer vegan aioli, replace the eggs and canola oil in the aioli recipe with 1 cup (8 fl oz/240 ml) vegan mayo, then continue to combine with the other ingredients as directed.

MUSHROOM BURGERS WITH DIJON AIOLI AND PICKLED RED ONIONS

SERVES 6

FOR THE MUSHROOM BURGERS

3 cloves garlic

1 lb (450 g) assorted mushrooms, such as portobello, king trumpet, and/or shiitake, stemmed (portobellos quartered)

1 small red onion, quartered

5 tablespoons (2½ fl oz/75 ml) neutral oil, such as canola, plus more as needed

1½ tablespoons Worcestershire sauce or vegan coconut aminos

1 tablespoon smoked paprika

Kosher salt and freshly ground pepper

1 cup (5½ oz/155 g) cooked brown rice

1 cup (3½ oz/100 g) panko bread crumbs

¼ cup (½ oz/15 g) chopped fresh flat-leaf parsley

2 tablespoons chopped fresh chives, cut into 1-inch (2.5-cm) pieces

Dijon Aioli (page 212)

6 hamburger buns or large lettuce leaves

Baby arugula

Sliced avocado

Pickled Red Onion (page 209)

Thinly sliced jalapeño chiles

To make the burgers, with a food processor running, drop in the garlic cloves and process until minced. Working in two batches, add the mushrooms and onion and process each addition until finely chopped.

In a large frying pan over medium-high heat, warm 2 tablespoons of the neutral oil. Add the mushroom mixture and cook, stirring occasionally and scraping up any browned bits, until the liquid released from the mushrooms has evaporated, 5–7 minutes. Add the Worcestershire, paprika, 1 tablespoon salt, and pepper to taste. Cook, stirring occasionally and scraping up any browned bits, until the mixture begins to brown slightly, about 5 minutes. Remove from the heat and let cool for 10 minutes, then transfer to a bowl.

To the bowl with the mushroom mixture, add the rice, panko, parsley, chives, and salt to taste. Stir until a cohesive mixture forms. Divide into 6 equal portions, each about 4 oz (115 g), and form into 3-inch (7.5-cm) patties. Place on a large plate or a baking sheet and refrigerate, uncovered, for at least 1 hour or up to overnight.

When ready to serve, heat a large nonstick frying pan over medium-high heat. Pour in the remaining 3 tablespoons neutral oil and heat until it starts to smoke. Add the burgers and cook until a deep brown crust forms, about 3 minutes. Carefully flip the burgers and cook until warmed through, about 3 minutes more, adding another 1 tablespoon or so of oil if needed to prevent sticking.

Spread the aioli on the bun bottoms then top with the burgers (alternatively, place the burgers on the lettuce and spread with aioli). Top with the arugula, avocado, pickled onions, and jalapeño. Close with the bun tops or more lettuce and serve.

During one of Belle's summer trips to Italy, no matter where she ate, stuffed squash blossoms were always on the menu. There are many variations, but this recipe is an ode to a favorite dish Belle enjoyed in Orvieto. Serve the blossoms as an appetizer to another recipe inspired by Belle's Italian travels, Strozzapreti Pomodoro with Pesto and Pecorino Sardo, on page 108. *Buon appetito!*

CHEESE-STUFFED FRIED SQUASH BLOSSOMS

MAKES 16 BLOSSOMS; 6-8 SERVINGS

1 cup (8 oz/225 g) fresh ricotta cheese

¼ cup (1¼ oz/35 g) crumbled blue cheese, such as Gorgonzola

1 teaspoon finely grated lemon zest, plus more for serving

Kosher salt and freshly ground pepper

16 squash blossoms, stamens and pistils removed

Oil for frying, such as canola

1¼ cups (5½ oz/150 g) all-purpose flour

½ teaspoon baking soda

1 bottle (12 fl oz/350 ml) lager beer, chilled

To make the filling, in a small bowl, stir together the ricotta, blue cheese, and lemon zest. Season with 1 teaspoon salt and a few generous grinds of pepper. Transfer to a piping bag with a ½-inch (12-mm) opening.

Line a baking sheet with parchment paper. Carefully pipe 1 heaping tablespoon of filling into the center of each squash blossom, then gently close the petals around the filling, meeting them at the top and twisting them together slightly to enclose the filling. Place the blossoms on the prepared baking sheet.

Fill a large, heavy-bottomed pot with 3 inches (7.5 cm) of oil (filling it no more than halfway full) and heat to 350°F (180°C) on a deep-frying thermometer. Line another baking sheet with paper towels.

While the oil heats, make the batter. In a bowl, whisk together the flour, 1½ teaspoons salt, and baking soda. Add the beer and whisk until smooth and no streaks of flour remain, being careful not to deflate the batter.

Working with 1 squash blossom at a time, submerge the filled blossom in the batter, letting any excess batter drip off. Carefully add the battered blossom to the oil. Repeat to dip and add more blossoms to the pot, making sure not to crowd the pot. Fry, turning once with tongs, until the squash blossoms are deep golden brown, about 1 minute on each side.

Using the tongs and a slotted spoon, transfer the blossoms to the paper towel-lined baking sheet. Sprinkle with salt and lemon zest and serve immediately.

This versatile dish can be served as a vegetarian main course or a side dish to roasted or grilled meats. We love pairing it with a green salad and our Pizza Stone Pita with Muhammara and Herbed Labneh (page 57). The whipped tahini makes a bit more than you might need but can be refrigerated and used as a dip for raw vegetables or toasted pita or drizzled over roasted vegetables.

ROASTED EGGPLANT WITH WHIPPED TAHINI

MAKES 4 SERVINGS

FOR THE GARLIC CRISPS
3 cloves garlic, thinly sliced

¼ cup (2 fl oz/60 ml) neutral oil, such as canola

Pinch of kosher salt

FOR THE EGGPLANT
2 Italian eggplants, each about ¾ lb (340 g), halved lengthwise

½ cup (4 fl oz/120 ml) extra-virgin olive oil

Kosher salt and freshly ground pepper

1 teaspoon cumin seeds

¼ cup (3 oz/90 g) pomegranate molasses, plus more as needed

Fresh thyme leaves, for garnish

FOR THE WHIPPED TAHINI
¾ cup (6½ oz/185 g) tahini

½ cup (4 fl oz/120 ml) water

¼ cup (2 fl oz/60 ml) fresh lemon juice

1 clove garlic, coarsely chopped

1 teaspoon kosher salt

Preheat the oven to 400°F (200°C). Line a baking sheet with parchment paper.

To make the garlic crisps, set a fine-mesh sieve over a heatproof bowl. In a small saucepan over medium heat, combine the garlic, oil, and salt. Heat until the garlic begins to simmer. Reduce the heat to medium-low and cook, stirring, until golden brown, about 2 minutes. Pour the garlic mixture into the sieve. Set the garlic chips aside. Reserve the garlicky oil for another use.

To make the eggplant, place the halves cut side up on the prepared baking sheet. Using a sharp paring knife, score the eggplant in a crosshatch pattern, with each cut about ½ inch (12 mm) apart, making sure not to cut through the skin of the eggplant. Brush the oil over the eggplant halves, allowing it to soak into the cuts. Season the eggplant with salt and sprinkle with the cumin seeds, making sure to season within the cuts. Brush the cut sides of the eggplant halves with a thin layer of the pomegranate molasses.

Roast the eggplant cut side up until very tender and caramelized on the surface, about 30 minutes. Every 10 minutes, brush the cut sides of the eggplant with another thin layer of pomegranate molasses. Once tender, remove the eggplant from the oven and let cool for 5 minutes.

Meanwhile, make the whipped tahini. In a blender, combine the tahini, water, lemon juice, garlic, and salt. Blend on high speed until well mixed, about 30 seconds. Pour into a bowl and set aside.

To serve, transfer the eggplant to a platter and drizzle with the whipped tahini. Top with the thyme and garlic chips and season with salt and pepper. Serve warm or at room temperature.

What's the secret to preparing potatoes that are tender on the inside and crispy on the outside? We use a two-step cooking process: first they're simmered on the stovetop and then they're roasted in the oven. To expose more of the surface area for crisping, we give them a gentle smash. And while the potatoes are practically perfect on their own, the accompanying garlicky aioli may be our favorite part. It's embellished with tender melted leeks, fresh tarragon, and a big squeeze of lemon juice, perfect for a spring or early-summer side.

ROASTED POTATOES WITH CHARRED LEEK AND TARRAGON AIOLI

MAKES 6 SERVINGS

FOR THE POTATOES

3 lb (1.4 kg) small yellow potatoes

Kosher salt and freshly ground pepper

⅓ cup (2¾ fl oz/80 ml) extra-virgin olive oil, plus more as needed

FOR THE LEEK AND TARRAGON AIOLI

¼ cup (2 fl oz/60 ml) extra-virgin olive oil

2 large or 6 small leeks, white and light green parts only, chopped

1 tablespoon unsalted butter

2 cloves garlic, minced

Kosher salt and freshly ground pepper

1 large egg plus 1 large egg yolk

1 cup (8 fl oz/240 ml) neutral oil, such as canola

1 teaspoon Dijon mustard

Juice of 1 lemon

1½ tablespoons chopped fresh tarragon

Chopped and whole fresh tarragon leaves, for garnish

Flake salt

Position 2 racks in the center of the oven and preheat the oven to 400°F (200°C).

Meanwhile, add the potatoes to a large pot of cold salted water and bring to a boil over high heat. Cook until fork-tender, 8–10 minutes. Drain and pat dry.

Divide the potatoes between 2 rimmed baking sheets and drizzle with the olive oil. Using your hands, coat the potatoes completely with the oil. Season generously with kosher salt and pepper. Roast until the potatoes are starting to brown, about 10 minutes, rotating the baking sheets between the racks halfway through.

Using the bottom of a measuring cup, carefully smash the potatoes until flattened slightly. If you can't easily smash them, return them to the oven and roast for about 5 minutes more.

Increase the oven temperature to 450°F (230°C). Return the smashed potatoes to the oven and roast until very crisp, about 15 minutes, rotating the baking sheets between the racks halfway through. If the potatoes look dry, drizzle with more olive oil.

While the potatoes are roasting, make the aioli. In a large frying pan over medium-high heat, warm the olive oil. Add the leeks and cook, stirring occasionally, until starting to soften and char, about 8 minutes. Add the butter and garlic and cook, stirring, until fragrant, about 1 minute. Reduce the heat to medium and cook, stirring occasionally, until the leeks are very soft, about 5 minutes. Remove from the heat and season to taste with kosher salt and pepper. Let cool.

Place the whole egg and egg yolk in a food processor and pulse to combine. With the machine running, slowly add a few drops of the neutral oil, then follow with a slow and steady stream of oil. Continue to blend until thoroughly combined and thickened. Transfer to a bowl and stir in the leek mixture, mustard, lemon juice, and tarragon. Season to taste with kosher salt and pepper. Set aside.

Spread the aioli on a plate or serving platter and top with the potatoes. Drizzle with olive oil, garnish with chopped and whole tarragon leaves, and sprinkle with flake salt. Serve immediately.

This is such a great side dish, we usually want to keep the whole plate to ourselves. Smashing and salting the cucumbers causes them to sweat a lot of their water, which allows the tender interior to better absorb our delicious vinaigrette flavored with mustard, garlic, honey, and chives. Serve these cucumbers with our Gochujang Chicken Thighs with Green Onion Slaw (page 134) or Chinese-Style Whole Fish with Ginger and Chili Crisp (page 135) and plenty of Lena's Chili Crisp (page 210) and steamed rice.

SMASHED CUCUMBERS WITH MUSTARD VINAIGRETTE

MAKES 2–4 SERVINGS

1 English cucumber (about 1 lb/450 g), trimmed and halved lengthwise

Kosher salt

FOR THE MUSTARD VINAIGRETTE
¼ cup (2 fl oz/60 ml) unseasoned rice vinegar

½ teaspoon grated garlic

1 tablespoon plus 1 teaspoon Dijon mustard

2 teaspoons whole-grain mustard

1 tablespoon plus 2 teaspoons honey, preferably local wildflower honey

2 tablespoons neutral oil, such as avocado

1 teaspoon yellow mustard seeds

½ teaspoon kosher salt

½ teaspoon freshly ground pepper

2 tablespoons chopped fresh chives

Flake salt, for garnish

Place the cucumber halves cut side down on a cutting board. Place the side of a large chef's knife over one edge of the cucumber and, using your palm, press the side of the knife against the edge, moving along the entire length of the cucumber until it splits (this might get messy). Slice the cucumber on the diagonal into 1-inch (2.5-cm) pieces.

Transfer the cucumber pieces to a fine-mesh sieve set over a bowl. Sprinkle 1 teaspoon kosher salt over the cucumber and toss to coat evenly. Let the cucumber drain for 20–30 minutes, giving the colander a few gentle shakes every 10 minutes to remove excess water.

Meanwhile, prepare the vinaigrette. In a bowl, combine the vinegar and garlic. Let stand for about 10 minutes to mellow out the raw bite of the garlic. Add the mustards and honey. Slowly add the oil, whisking constantly until well blended. Stir in the mustard seeds, kosher salt, and pepper. Cover and refrigerate until ready to serve.

Transfer the cucumber to a serving bowl, add the chives, and toss with about one-third of the vinaigrette. Sprinkle with flake salt and serve, passing the remainder of the vinaigrette alongside.

Cauliflower has become the superstar of the vegetable world in recent years. Its mild flavor makes an excellent blank canvas for nearly any spice and herb. Here we toss cauliflower florets with harissa, a North African hot chili powder that toasts to perfection in the oven. To balance the heat, the cauliflower is served with *labneh*, a creamy, tangy soft cheese made from yogurt. The dish is finished with crispy green onions and pickled red onions for more bursts of fresh flavor.

HARISSA CAULIFLOWER WITH CRISPY GREEN ONIONS, LABNEH, AND PICKLED RED ONION

MAKES 4 SERVINGS

FOR THE CAULIFLOWER
1 head cauliflower, cut into florets

5 tablespoons (2½ fl oz/75 ml) extra-virgin olive oil

4 teaspoons harissa spice powder

½ teaspoon kosher salt

FOR THE CRISPY GREEN ONIONS
¼ cup (2 fl oz/60 ml) extra-virgin olive oil

1 bunch green onions, trimmed and sliced crosswise

Kosher salt

FOR SERVING
1 cup (8 oz/225 g) labneh, at room temperature

Watercress (optional)

Pickled Red Onion (page 209)

Flake salt

Preheat the oven to 425°F (220°C).

To make the cauliflower, in a large bowl, combine the cauliflower, oil, harissa powder, and kosher salt. Toss until the cauliflower is evenly coated. Transfer to a rimmed baking sheet and spread into an even layer. Roast, tossing with tongs once halfway through roasting, until the cauliflower is charred and tender, 30–35 minutes.

Meanwhile, make the crispy green onions. In a frying pan over medium-high heat, warm the oil. Add the green onions and cook, stirring occasionally, until softened, about 45 seconds. Reduce the heat to medium and cook, stirring occasionally, until the green onions are crisp but have not turned brown, 2–3 minutes. Sprinkle with kosher salt.

To serve, spread the labneh on a serving platter. Top with watercress (if using), then the cauliflower, crispy green onions and accumulated oil, and pickled onions. Sprinkle everything with flake salt. Serve immediately.

A confit refers to any type of food that is preserved by means of cooking it low and slow in a liquid—typically fat. Here, cherry tomatoes are cooked in really good extra-virgin olive oil with balsamic, garlic, and rosemary until meltingly tender. The tomato confit is then served with fluffy ricotta and crunchy toasts. We think this dish is best served family-style as a hearty appetizer with a bottle of red or a round of our La Dolce Vita Spritz (page 18).

TOMATO AND GARLIC CONFIT WITH WHIPPED RICOTTA AND TOASTED SOURDOUGH

MAKES 6-8 SERVINGS

FOR THE TOMATO CONFIT
1½ cups (12 fl oz/350 ml) high-quality extra-virgin olive oil

1 tablespoon balsamic vinegar

1 tablespoon kosher salt

2 lb (1 kg) cherry tomatoes

2 heads garlic, top 1 inch (2.5 cm) sliced off

5 fresh rosemary sprigs

FOR THE WHIPPED RICOTTA
2 cups (1 lb/450 g) whole-milk ricotta cheese

1 tablespoon heavy cream (optional)

1½ teaspoons kosher salt

Freshly ground pepper

Extra-virgin olive oil

1 loaf artisanal sourdough bread, cut into 10 slices each 1 inch (2.5 cm) thick

Flake salt

To make the tomato confit, preheat the oven to 250°F (120°C). In a bowl, whisk together the olive oil, balsamic, and salt. Arrange the tomatoes, garlic heads (cut side up), and rosemary sprigs in an even layer in a 9-by-13-inch (23-by-33-cm) baking dish. Pour in the olive oil mixture and stir to coat. Bake, uncovered, until the tomatoes and garlic have softened and are very tender, about 2 hours.

Meanwhile, make the whipped ricotta. In a food processor, combine the ricotta, cream (if using), salt, and a few generous grinds of pepper and process on high for 2 minutes. Transfer to a serving bowl.

Just before serving, in a large nonstick frying pan over medium heat, warm 1 tablespoon oil. In batches, add the bread slices in a single layer and toast, turning once, until golden brown and crisp on both sides, about 1 minute per side. Transfer to a serving plate. Repeat with the remaining bread slices, adding oil to the pan as needed.

Transfer the tomato confit to a serving dish, discarding the rosemary sprigs. Gently press the garlic cloves out of their skin and add to the tomatoes.

To serve, spread the whipped ricotta on the toasted bread, then top with the tomato confit, garlic, and a sprinkle of flake salt.

TIP You can make the tomato confit ahead of time and store it in the fridge for up to 1 month. When ready to serve, let it come to room temperature or simmer gently over low heat.

White miso gives this easy dish a mild, mellow umami flavor. We pair the soybean paste with mirin, sake, and brown sugar in a glaze that delivers savory and caramelized notes to the roasted sweet potatoes. The result is a showstopping side for nearly any meal.

MISO-GLAZED SWEET POTATOES WITH GREEN ONIONS AND SESAME

MAKES 4-6 SERVINGS

5 small Japanese sweet potatoes or 3 medium Jewel yams, halved lengthwise

2 tablespoons neutral oil, such as avocado

Kosher salt

3 tablespoons sake

3 tablespoons mirin

½ cup (4 oz/115 g) white miso

¼ cup (2 oz/60 g) firmly packed light brown sugar

2 green onions, thinly sliced on the diagonal, for serving

1 tablespoon sesame seeds, for serving

Preheat the oven to 425°F (220°C). Line a large baking sheet with parchment paper.

In a large bowl, combine the sweet potatoes, oil, and a large pinch of salt. Toss to coat evenly. Arrange in a single layer cut side down on the prepared baking sheet. Roast until the sweet potatoes are very tender, 20-40 minutes, depending on the size of the sweet potatoes.

Meanwhile, make the glaze. In a small saucepan over low heat, combine the sake, mirin, miso, and brown sugar. Whisk until smooth and slightly thickened, 3-4 minutes.

Remove the sweet potatoes from the oven, turn cut side up, and generously brush with half of the glaze. Continue to roast until the sweet potatoes are extremely soft and fall out of their skin, 5-10 minutes longer.

Glaze the sweet potatoes with the remaining glaze. Carefully position a rack 4 inches (10 cm) from the broiler and turn the oven on to broil. Return the sweet potatoes to the oven and broil until charred, watching closely to prevent too much browning, 2-3 more minutes.

Transfer the sweet potatoes to a serving plate, garnish with the green onions and sesame seeds, and serve immediately.

Indulge your cravings for deep-fried, salty dishes with healthier versions using an air fryer. Here, both chickpeas and sweet potatoes are air fried until they are crisp on the outside and tender on the inside. Then they are layered with lettuce, feta, jalapeños, and pickled onions for a hearty snack or vegetarian meal that's equal parts crispy, creamy, tangy, and spicy.

LOADED SWEET POTATO FRIES

MAKES 4–6 SERVINGS

FOR THE AIR-FRIED CHICKPEAS
1 can (14 oz/400 g) chickpeas, drained, rinsed, and dried

2 tablespoons extra-virgin olive oil

Kosher salt and freshly ground pepper

FOR THE SWEET POTATO FRIES
2 teaspoons ground sumac

2 teaspoons smoked paprika

2 teaspoons ground cumin

2 teaspoons kosher salt

1 teaspoon freshly ground pepper

2 lb (1 kg) sweet potatoes, cut into ½-inch-thick (12-mm) batons

FOR ASSEMBLING
1 head romaine lettuce, thinly sliced

2 oz (60 g) feta cheese, crumbled

2 tablespoons pepitas, toasted

1 jalapeño chile, thinly sliced into rounds

Pickled Red Onion (page 209)

½ cup (4 oz/115 g) sour cream

Freshly ground pepper

To make the air-fried chickpeas, preheat an air fryer to 450°F (230°C) according to the manufacturer's instructions. In a bowl, combine the chickpeas and olive oil. Season with salt and pepper to taste and toss to coat the chickpeas. Spread in an even layer in the air fryer basket. Cook until the skin of the chickpeas has split and they are crisp and browned, about 15 minutes. Transfer to a bowl and set aside.

Lower the air fryer temperature to 400°F (200°C).

To make the sweet potato fries, in a small bowl, stir together the sumac, paprika, cumin, salt, and pepper. Put the sweet potatoes into a large bowl and spray with a generous amount of olive oil spray. Sprinkle the spice mixture over the sweet potatoes and toss to coat. Spread in an even layer in the air fryer basket and cook until the sweet potatoes are crispy on the outside and tender on the inside, 15–20 minutes.

To assemble, arrange the romaine on a serving platter. Scatter the sweet potato fries on top, followed by the chickpeas. Sprinkle the feta, pepitas, and jalapeño evenly on top and add as many of the pickled onions as you like. Dollop evenly with the sour cream, season with pepper, and serve.

DESSERTS

Whether you're hosting a dinner party or cooking a cozy dinner for two, this gluten-free chocolate cake wraps up the night flawlessly. It's a dessert that seems fancy but calls for just a handful of common ingredients and is quite easy to make. Consider this a blank canvas for your favorite dessert toppings. Here, we serve it dusted with confectioners' sugar and accompanied with whipped cream, but it is also wonderful topped with ice cream, caramel sauce, or a ton of fresh berries.

FLOURLESS CHOCOLATE CAKE

MAKES 8 SERVINGS

½ cup (4 oz/115 g) unsalted butter, at room temperature, cut into pieces, plus more for the pan

10 oz (285 g) semisweet chocolate chips

5 large eggs, separated

1 tablespoon pure vanilla extract

¾ teaspoon kosher salt

½ cup (3½ oz/100 g) granulated sugar

Confectioners' sugar or cocoa powder, for dusting (optional)

Whipped cream (page 213), for serving (optional)

Preheat the oven to 275°F (135°C). Butter a 9-inch (23-cm) springform pan. Line the bottom with a parchment paper circle. Butter the paper.

Fill a small saucepan with 1 inch (2.5 cm) of water and place over medium heat. Place a large heatproof bowl on top, making sure the bottom of the bowl is not touching the water. Add the butter and chocolate chips to the bowl and melt, stirring occasionally. Remove the bowl and set aside to cool slightly, then whisk the egg yolks, vanilla, and salt into the chocolate mixture. Set aside.

In the bowl of a stand mixer fitted with the whisk attachment (or using a handheld beater), beat the egg whites on medium-high speed until soft peaks form, about 1 minute. Reduce the speed to medium and slowly add the granulated sugar to the egg whites, beating until stiff glossy peaks form, about 1 minute more. Transfer the whipped egg whites to the chocolate mixture and gently fold to combine until no streaks remain.

Pour the batter into the prepared pan and spread into an even layer. Bake until the cake puffs up, forms a crust, and is beginning to pull away from the sides of the pan, about 45 minutes. Transfer to a wire rack to cool.

Once the cake is completely cool, remove the sides of the pan and slide (or use a spatula to guide) the cake onto a serving platter. If desired, dust with confectioners' sugar and serve with whipped cream.

When it comes to no-bake desserts, chocolate mousse is one of our favorites. It's rich, flavorful, and can be made in advance. The texture of a mousse varies depending on the preparation. Some are thick and creamy, but ours is light and fluffy, thanks to the whipped egg whites and cream, which incorporate a lot of air into the chocolate base. You can eat it straight up, but we love the combination of raspberries and chocolate, and the light sprinkle of flake salt balances the flavors beautifully.

RICH CHOCOLATE MOUSSE

MAKES 6 SERVINGS

7 oz (200 g) bittersweet chocolate, preferably 74 percent cacao

3 tablespoons unsalted butter

3 large eggs, separated

½ teaspoon cream of tartar

⅛ teaspoon kosher salt

¼ cup (1¾ oz/50 g) plus 1 tablespoon sugar

½ cup (4 fl oz/120 ml) heavy cream

½ teaspoon pure vanilla extract

⅛ teaspoon ground cinnamon, preferably Ceylon

Flake salt, for garnish

Fresh raspberries, for garnish

In a heatproof bowl set over (but not touching) barely simmering water in a saucepan, heat the chocolate and butter, stirring, until melted, 2–3 minutes. Remove the bowl from the saucepan and set aside to cool to room temperature, about 7 minutes.

While the chocolate mixture cools, in the bowl of a stand mixer fitted with the whisk attachment (or using a handheld mixer), beat the egg whites, cream of tartar, and salt on medium-high speed until soft peaks form, about 2 minutes. Gradually add ¼ cup (1¾ oz/50 g) of the sugar and continue beating until stiff peaks form, about 2 more minutes.

Whisk the egg yolks into the cooled chocolate mixture one at a time. Using a large rubber spatula, gently fold the egg whites into the chocolate mixture just until smooth. Set aside.

In the clean bowl of the stand mixer fitted with the whisk attachment (or using a handheld mixer), beat the cream on medium-high speed until it begins to thicken. Add the remaining 1 tablespoon sugar, the vanilla, and cinnamon and continue to beat until the cream holds medium peaks, about 2 minutes. Fold the whipped cream into the chocolate mixture until just incorporated. Do not overmix.

Divide the mousse among six 3-fl oz (90-ml) ramekins. Cover and refrigerate for at least 2 hours or up to 4 days. Just before serving, garnish with flake salt and raspberries.

Citrus is at its prime in the winter months, so we love to use all the wonderful varieties in all the wonderful ways—including this upside-down cake, which has an almond flour–based batter and is topped with lightly sweetened labneh, a soft Middle Eastern cheese that we have used in a few savory recipes in this book. The flavor is reminiscent of a Creamsicle, while the presentation is a sophisticated showstopper. We incorporate two varieties of orange, a grapefruit, and kumquats in this seasonal cake. There is no need to peel the kumquats; their peel is tender enough to eat and is the source of their sweet flavor.

WINTER CITRUS UPSIDE-DOWN CAKE

MAKES 6–8 SERVINGS

FOR THE CITRUS CAKE
1½ cups (10½ oz/300 g) sugar

¼ cup (2 fl oz/60 ml) water

1 blood orange, peeled and cut into rounds ¼ inch (6 mm) thick

1 navel orange, peeled and cut into rounds ¼ inch (6 mm) thick

1 small grapefruit, peeled and cut into rounds ¼ inch (6 mm) thick

8 kumquats, cut into rounds ½ inch (12 mm) thick

1 cup (3½ oz/100 g) almond flour

⅔ cup (3 oz/80 g) all-purpose flour

1¼ teaspoons baking powder

½ teaspoon kosher salt

11 tablespoons (5½ oz/155 g) unsalted butter, at room temperature

3 large eggs, beaten

1 tablespoon finely grated navel orange zest

1 tablespoon fresh navel orange juice

2 teaspoons pure vanilla extract

To make the cake, preheat the oven to 375°F (190°C). Line the bottom of an 8- or 9-inch (20- or 23-cm) square cake pan with parchment paper. Spray the bottom and sides of the pan with cooking spray.

In a small saucepan over medium-high heat, combine ½ cup (3½ oz/100 g) of the sugar and the water and bring to a simmer, whisking until the sugar is completely dissolved. Pour half of this syrup into the prepared pan. Arrange the oranges, grapefruit, and kumquat slices over the syrup, using half and partial pieces to fill in the gaps. Pour the remaining syrup over the citrus. Set aside.

In a medium bowl, whisk together both flours, the baking powder, and salt. Set aside.

In the bowl of a stand mixer fitted with the paddle attachment, beat together the butter and the remaining 1 cup (7 oz/200 g) sugar on medium-high speed until light and fluffy, about 2 minutes. Add the eggs and beat until combined, stopping the mixer to scrape down the sides of the bowl as needed. Add the orange zest and juice and vanilla and beat until combined, about 10 seconds. Stop the mixer and scrape down the sides of the bowl. With the mixer on medium-low speed, add the flour mixture in two additions and beat until just combined.

Continues on next page

Continued from previous page

FOR THE SWEETENED LABNEH
⅔ cup (5½ oz/155 g) labneh

2 tablespoons sugar

1 tablespoon heavy cream

Pour the batter over the citrus in the pan and spread evenly. Bake until a toothpick inserted into the center of the cake comes out clean, 40–45 minutes, covering the pan loosely with aluminum foil if the cake starts to brown too quickly. Transfer the pan to a wire rack and let cool for about 20 minutes, then invert the cake onto a cake plate. Let cool for 10 minutes more.

Meanwhile, make the sweetened labneh. In a small bowl, whisk together the labneh, sugar, and cream until very smooth.

Cut the cake into slices and serve warm or at room temperature with the sweetened labneh.

Inspired by sweet Maine blueberries, this cake is the perfect ending to any meal. Unlike most cakes, where a sunken middle means something went wrong, this cake is meant to cave in and create the perfect crater for the mascarpone whipped cream. The soft Italian cheese has a tang similar to American cream cheese, but it is much richer and the perfect balancing act to a sweet cake like this one.

SUNKEN BLUEBERRY CAKE WITH MASCARPONE WHIPPED CREAM

MAKES 6-8 SERVINGS

FOR THE BLUEBERRY CAKE

3 large eggs, at room temperature

½ cup (3½ oz/100 g) plus 1 teaspoon granulated sugar

1 cup (8 oz/225 g) whole-milk ricotta cheese

1 cup (8 oz/225 g) sour cream

6 tablespoons (3 oz/90 g) unsalted butter, melted and cooled slightly

1 tablespoon finely grated lemon zest

½ teaspoon pure vanilla extract

½ teaspoon pure almond extract

1 cup (4¼ oz/120 g) all-purpose flour

1 teaspoon baking powder

1 teaspoon kosher salt

2 cups (10 oz/285 g) fresh blueberries

1 teaspoon fresh lemon juice

Confectioners' sugar, for dusting

FOR THE MASCARPONE WHIPPED CREAM

1 cup (8 fl oz/240 ml) heavy cream

½ cup (4¼ oz/125 g) mascarpone cheese

3 tablespoons granulated sugar

1 teaspoon pure vanilla extract

To make the cake, preheat the oven to 375°F (190°C). Generously grease an 8-inch (20-cm) round cake pan with cooking spray.

In the bowl of a stand mixer fitted with the whisk attachment, combine the eggs and ½ cup (3½ oz/100 g) of the granulated sugar. Beat on medium speed until the mixture thickens and turns pale, 4-5 minutes. Reduce the speed to low, then add the ricotta, sour cream, butter, lemon zest, and vanilla and almond extracts. Beat until combined, about 30 seconds. Add the flour, baking powder, and salt and beat until just combined, about 15 seconds. Increase the mixer speed to medium-high and beat for 1 minute more.

Pour the batter into the prepared pan and spread evenly. Top the batter with 1½ cups (7½ oz/210 g) of the blueberries, concentrating them in the center of the cake.

Bake until the edge of the cake is golden brown, about 40 minutes. The cake should be set but still jiggle slightly in the center. Transfer to a wire rack and let cool for 20 minutes.

In a small bowl, toss the remaining ½ cup (2½ oz/70 g) blueberries with the lemon juice and remaining 1 teaspoon granulated sugar. Set aside.

To make the mascarpone whipped cream, in the clean bowl of the stand mixer fitted with the whisk attachment, beat the cream on medium speed until soft peaks form, 1-2 minutes. Add the cheese, granulated sugar, and vanilla and beat until medium peaks form, 8-10 seconds.

To serve, pile the sugared blueberries in the center of the cake. Dust the edges of the cake with confectioners' sugar. Cut the cake into wedges and serve with the mascarpone whipped cream alongside.

We *love love love* this cheesecake! Originating in San Sebastian, Spain—a favorite culinary destination of ours—this version is not only made without a crust but is also baked at a higher temperature than most cheesecakes, so it ends up dark and toasted on the outside and smooth and custardy on the inside. We season our version with warming spices—ginger, cinnamon, and cloves—making this a wonderful dessert for the fall and winter months. It's great when you're entertaining because both the cheesecake and the caramel sauce can be made in advance. Then, just before serving, whip the cream, spread it on the cake, pour on the sauce, and serve.

BASQUE CHEESECAKE WITH SALTED BRANDY-CARAMEL SAUCE

MAKES 10-12 SERVINGS

FOR THE BASQUE CHEESECAKE
2 lb (1 kg) cream cheese,
at room temperature

1⅓ cups (9½ oz/270 g) sugar

6 large eggs

2 cups (16 fl oz/475 ml) heavy cream

2 teaspoons pure vanilla extract

2 teaspoons ground ginger

2 teaspoons ground cinnamon

1 teaspoon ground cloves

1 teaspoon kosher salt

⅓ cup (1½ oz/40 g) all-purpose flour

**FOR THE SALTED
BRANDY-CARAMEL SAUCE**
1 cup (7 oz/200 g) sugar

¼ cup (2 fl oz/60 ml) water

2 teaspoons light corn syrup

½ cup (4 fl oz/120 ml) heavy cream

¼ cup (2 fl oz/60 ml) brandy

¼ teaspoon kosher salt

Whipped Cream (page 213), for serving

To make the cheesecake, preheat the oven to 400°F (200°C). Coat a 10-inch (25-cm) springform pan with cooking spray, then line with parchment paper, pressing the parchment up the sides of the pan.

In the bowl of a stand mixer fitted with the paddle attachment, beat the cream cheese on medium speed until smooth, about 1 minute. Stop the mixer and scrape down the sides of the bowl. Add the sugar and beat on medium speed until very smooth, about 2 minutes. Add the eggs one at a time and beat after each addition until well mixed, about 1 minute. Reduce the speed to medium-low, add the cream, vanilla, ginger, cinnamon, cloves, and salt, and beat after each addition until well mixed, about 30 seconds, stopping to scrape down the sides of the bowl as needed.

Remove the bowl from the mixer stand and sift the flour over the top. Using a rubber spatula, fold in the flour until just combined and no dry streaks remain; be sure to use a light touch so the batter doesn't deflate. Pour the batter into the prepared pan and spread evenly.

Bake until the cheesecake is deeply browned but still jiggles in the center, about 1 hour. It will seem underdone but will continue to set as it cools and falls.

Transfer the pan to a wire rack and let the cheesecake cool in the pan for 20 minutes. Using a small offset spatula or a table knife, loosen the cheesecake from the sides of the pan, then remove the outer ring. Let cool completely at room temperature, or cover and refrigerate for at least 30 minutes or up to overnight. Before serving, carefully transfer the cake to a serving plate.

Meanwhile, make the caramel sauce. In a saucepan over medium heat, combine the sugar, water, and corn syrup. Bring to a simmer and cook, without stirring to prevent crystallization, until deep amber, about 6 minutes. Occasionally swirl the pan gently for even cooking. Watch closely so the mixture doesn't burn. Remove from the heat.

While whisking constantly, slowly and carefully add the cream; the mixture will boil vigorously. When the boiling subsides, whisk until smooth. Whisk in the brandy and salt, then set the pan over medium heat and cook, stirring, for 1 minute. Remove from the heat and let cool for 10 minutes.

Transfer the sauce to a heatproof container and let cool for 30 minutes to thicken. Use immediately, or cover and refrigerate for up to 1 week. If refrigerated, bring the sauce to room temperature or heat in a warm water bath before using.

To serve, spread the whipped cream over the cheesecake, then pour the caramel sauce over the top. Cut into slices and serve.

Belle wasn't sure that she could improve on her classic chocolate chip cookie recipe, which she has been perfecting since she was ten years old, but after countless tests, these beautifully marbled cookies are her new favorite. The Dutch-process cocoa imparts an intense chocolaty flavor, while the bread flour gives the cookies just the right amount of chewiness. For the best results, use a kitchen scale to weigh the flour, chocolate, and other ingredients, then again to help you evenly divide the dough as instructed. Belle likes them warm right off the pan with a glass of milk, but Devon prefers when they are fully cooled and even a day or two old since they have had more time to develop their flavor. But however—and whenever—you eat them, you will love them. We promise.

MARBLED CHOCOLATE CHIP COOKIES

MAKES 8 LARGE COOKIES

1⅓ cups (6 oz/160 g)
plus 3½ tablespoons bread flour

1 teaspoon baking powder

1 teaspoon baking soda

1 teaspoon kosher salt

½ cup (4 oz/115 g) unsalted butter,
at room temperature

½ cup (3½ oz/100 g) firmly packed
dark brown sugar

6 tablespoons (3 oz/90 g)
granulated sugar

1 large egg, at room temperature

1½ tablespoons vanilla bean paste
or pure vanilla extract

1 cup (6 oz/170g) dark chocolate chips
(preferably 70 percent cacao)

3 tablespoons Dutch-process
cocoa powder

Position 1 rack in the upper third and 1 rack in the lower third of the oven and preheat to 350°F (180°C). Line 2 baking sheets with parchment paper.

In a medium bowl, whisk together 1⅓ cups (6 oz/160 g) plus 2 tablespoons of the flour, the baking powder, baking soda, and salt. Set aside.

In the bowl of a stand mixer fitted with the paddle attachment, beat together the butter, brown sugar, and granulated sugar on medium-high speed until light and fluffy, about 2 minutes, stopping the mixer to scrape down the sides of the bowl as needed. Add the egg and vanilla and beat on medium speed until combined, about 30 seconds. With the mixer running on low speed, slowly add the flour mixture, then increase the speed to medium and beat until combined, about 1 minute.

Transfer half of the dough to a medium bowl. Add the remaining 1½ tablespoons flour to the dough in this bowl. Using a rubber spatula, fold in the flour until combined, then fold in ½ cup (3 oz/85 g) of the chocolate chips. This is the vanilla dough. Set aside.

To the remaining dough in the mixer bowl, add the cocoa powder and beat on medium speed until combined, about 1 minute. Using a rubber spatula, fold in the remaining ½ cup (3 oz/85 g) chocolate chips. This is the chocolate dough.

Continues on next page

Continued from previous page

Divide each dough into 16 equal portions, each weighing about ¾ oz (20 g). Using the palms of your hands, roll 2 portions of vanilla dough and 2 portions of chocolate dough together into a ball so they slightly marble into each other. Split the ball of dough in half with your fingers, rotate one of the halves vertically 180 degrees, and press the flat sides back together. Briefly roll again between your palms. Repeat 2–3 times more until the desired marbling is achieved. Repeat with the remaining portions of dough to form a total of 8 cookies. Arrange 4 dough balls on each prepared baking sheet, spacing them about 3 inches (7.5 cm) apart.

Bake the cookies for 5 minutes, then remove the baking sheets from the oven and gently bang the sheets on a heatproof surface once or twice; the cookies should deflate slightly. Return them to the oven, rotating the sheets between the racks and from front to back. Bake until the cookies are set, 4–6 minutes more. Let the cookies cool on the baking sheets on wire racks for 5 minutes, then transfer the cookies to the racks to cool. Serve warm or at room temperature.

Oh, the joys of the Test Kitchen. One time when we baked really good snickerdoodles, we decided they would be even better paired with a spoonful of peanut butter. So we pulled out the jar of PB and proved ourselves right. Next, Belle figured out how to incorporate the PB into the batter without compromising the integrity of the iconic snickerdoodle texture—a little extra baking soda did the trick. After a few rounds, she got here: a hybrid of a classic peanut butter cookie with the puffy nature of a snickerdoodle. Eat warm off the baking sheet paired with a tall glass of cold milk for the full experience.

CHEWY PEANUT BUTTER SNICKERDOODLES

MAKES 12 COOKIES

1½ cups (6½ oz/180 g) all-purpose flour

1 teaspoon baking soda

¼ teaspoon kosher salt

½ cup (4 oz/115 g) unsalted butter, at room temperature

1 cup (10 oz/285 g) creamy peanut butter

¾ cup (5¼ oz/150 g) granulated sugar

¾ cup (5½ oz/155 g) firmly packed dark brown sugar

1 large egg, at room temperature

2 teaspoons pure vanilla extract

1½ teaspoons ground cinnamon

Position 1 rack in the upper third and 1 rack in the lower third of the oven and preheat to 350°F (180°C). Line 2 baking sheets with parchment paper.

In a medium bowl, whisk together the flour, baking soda, and salt. Set aside. In the bowl of a stand mixer fitted with the paddle attachment (or using a handheld mixer), beat the butter, peanut butter, ¼ cup (1¾ oz/50 g) of the granulated sugar, and the brown sugar on medium-high speed until smooth, creamy, and light brown, about 1 minute. Stop the mixer and scrape down the sides of the bowl. Add the egg and vanilla and beat on medium speed until just combined, then add the flour mixture and beat on low speed just until combined.

In a medium bowl, whisk together the remaining ½ cup (3½ oz/100 g) granulated sugar and the cinnamon until combined.

For each cookie, scoop up a spoonful of dough (about 2 oz/60 g) and form into a 2-inch (5-cm) ball. Roll each ball in the cinnamon sugar to coat completely. Arrange 6 dough balls at least 3 inches (7.5 cm) apart on each prepared baking sheet for a total of 12 cookies.

Bake until the cookies are slightly cracked on top and light golden brown, about 13 minutes, rotating the baking sheets between the racks and from front to back halfway through baking.

Bang the baking sheets gently on the counter to deflate the cookies slightly, then let cool on the baking sheets on wire racks for 5 minutes. Using a spatula, transfer the cookies to the racks. Serve warm or at room temperature.

Devon sought to create a grain-free and refined sugar-free version of our favorite classic cookie. After lots of tests, she found that the combination of almond and cassava flours provided the most structure without any unpleasant aftertaste. Solid coconut oil had enough body to cream with the coconut sugar, trapping air as butter would to ensure good texture in the finished cookie. And since we omitted the gluten, adding an egg and a bit of almond milk was a crucial step in getting all the ingredients to bind to form a dough. From there, we added vanilla, chocolate chips, and salt and finally arrived where we wanted to be—in a land where cookies are filled with wholesome ingredients but are still delicious and nostalgic.

GRAIN-FREE CHOCOLATE CHIP COOKIES

MAKES 8 LARGE COOKIES

2 cups (7 oz/200 g) almond flour

½ cup (2¾ oz/80 g) cassava flour

¾ teaspoon baking soda

½ teaspoon baking powder

1 teaspoon kosher salt

⅓ cup (2½ oz/70 g) solid coconut oil

¾ cup (5 oz/140 g) coconut sugar

1 tablespoon vanilla bean paste or pure vanilla extract

1 large egg

2 tablespoons almond milk

¼ lb (115 g) dark chocolate disks or chips

Flake salt (optional)

In a bowl, whisk together the almond flour, cassava flour, baking soda, baking powder, and salt. Set aside.

In the bowl of a stand mixer fitted with the paddle attachment, beat the coconut oil, coconut sugar, and vanilla on medium speed until well mixed, about 1 minute. Add the egg and beat on low until just combined, then beat in the almond milk.

With the mixer on low speed, slowly add the dry ingredients, beating until incorporated. Increase the speed to medium-high and beat until no streaks of flour remain, about 15 seconds. Fold in the chocolate disks. Cover and refrigerate for 30 minutes.

While the dough chills, preheat the oven to 350°F (180°C). Line 2 baking sheets with parchment paper.

Using your hands, form the dough into 2-inch (5-cm) balls, then arrange the balls on the prepared baking sheets, spacing them at least 2 inches (5 cm) apart. Using a palm, press the dough into disks ½ inch (12 mm) thick. Sprinkle the cookies generously with flake salt if desired.

Bake until the cookies are golden brown, about 12 minutes. Let cool on the baking sheets on wire racks for 5 minutes, then transfer to the racks to cool. Serve warm or at room temperature.

Is there anything better than a chocolate chip cookie? What about a giant one baked in a cast-iron frying pan and designed to be devoured straight from the pan? That's what we thought. Refrigerating the cookie dough prevents the cookie from spreading too much because the fat is colder and the sugar has time to absorb some of the liquid in the dough. It also results in a cookie that's perfectly browned with crispy edges and a soft, chewy center. The choice of chocolate—semisweet or bittersweet, in bars or disks—is up to you. Just make sure it is a top-quality brand, such as Guittard or Valrhona. A sprinkle of flake salt on the top of the cookie just before it goes into the oven will heighten the rich chocolate flavor. And although we like to top our giant cookie with vanilla ice cream, other flavors—mint chip, salted caramel, pistachio—would also be good. Get your spoons ready!

SKILLET CHOCOLATE CHIP COOKIE

MAKES 6–8 SERVINGS

1½ cups (6½ oz/180 g) all-purpose flour

1 teaspoon baking soda

1½ teaspoons kosher salt

½ cup (4 oz/115 g) unsalted butter, at room temperature

½ cup (3½ oz/100 g) granulated sugar

½ cup (3½ oz/100 g) firmly packed dark brown sugar

1 large egg

2 teaspoons vanilla bean paste or pure vanilla extract

½ lb (225 g) semisweet or bittersweet bar chocolate, roughly chopped, or chocolate disks

Vanilla ice cream, for serving

Preheat the oven to 350°F (180°C). Grease an 8- or 10-inch (20- or 25-cm) cast-iron frying pan with cooking spray.

In a medium bowl, combine the flour, baking soda, and salt. In the bowl of a stand mixer fitted with the paddle attachment, beat the butter on medium speed until smooth, about 1 minute. Add the sugars and beat on medium-high speed until light and fluffy, about 2 minutes. Add the egg and vanilla bean paste and beat on medium-high speed until just combined, about 30 seconds. Scrape down the sides of the bowl. In a few additions, add the dry ingredients, beating on medium-low speed until just combined. Finally, add the chocolate and beat on medium speed until just combined.

Transfer the dough to the prepared pan and spread into an even layer. If you have time, cover the dough with plastic wrap and refrigerate for 30 minutes or up to 2 days.

Bake until the edges are set but the center still jiggles slightly, 35–40 minutes for the 8-inch (20-cm) pan and 25–30 minutes for the 10-inch (25-cm) pan.

Let cool in the pan on a wire rack for 10 minutes, then top with scoops of vanilla ice cream and serve with spoons.

STOCKS, SAUCES, DRESSINGS & MORE

CHICKEN STOCK

MAKES ABOUT 2 QT (64 FL OZ/1.9 L)

6 lb (2.7 kg) chicken parts,
such as necks, wings, and/or drumsticks

2 large onions, roughly chopped

4 carrots, chopped

4 celery stalks, chopped

6 cloves garlic, crushed

1 bunch fresh herbs, such as parsley, dill,
and/or cilantro, leaves and tender stems

6 fresh thyme or rosemary sprigs

3 bay leaves

1 tablespoon black peppercorns

1 tablespoon kosher salt

3 qt (96 fl oz/2.8 l) water

In a large stockpot, combine all the ingredients, adding more water if needed to cover by 1 inch (2.5 cm). Bring to a boil over medium-high heat. Reduce the heat to low and simmer gently, uncovered and without stirring, for 4 hours. Skim off any foam or scum from the surface at the beginning of cooking.

Strain the stock through a fine-mesh sieve set over a large bowl. Press on the solids to extract as many cooking juices as possible, then discard the solids. Let cool completely. Transfer the stock to airtight containers and refrigerate until completely chilled, 4–8 hours, depending on the size of your containers.

Once the stock has chilled, skim off and discard the congealed fat from the surface. Refrigerate for up to 1 week or freeze for up to 3 months.

VEGETABLE STOCK

MAKES ABOUT 2 QT (64 FL OZ/1.9 L)

2 large leeks, trimmed

2 large carrots, sliced

2 large celery stalks, sliced

2 large yellow onions, sliced

3 cloves garlic, unpeeled

3 fresh flat-leaf parsley sprigs

2 fresh thyme sprigs

1 bay leaf

2 qt (64 fl oz/1.9 l) water

½ teaspoon black peppercorns

Kosher salt

Slice the white portion of the leeks and place in a large stockpot; reserve the green tops. Add the carrots, celery, onions, and garlic to the pot. Using kitchen string, tie together the reserved green leek tops with the parsley and thyme sprigs and bay leaf. Add to the pot along with the water.

Place over medium-low heat and bring slowly to a simmer, regularly skimming off the scum that rises to the surface until no more forms. Add the peppercorns, cover partially, and continue simmering for 1–1½ hours.

Line a large fine-mesh sieve with a double layer of dampened cheesecloth and set it inside a large heatproof bowl. Pour the contents of the pot into the sieve, then discard the solids. Season with salt and let cool to room temperature. Refrigerate in airtight containers for up to 5 days or freeze for up to 6 months.

FISH STOCK

MAKES ABOUT 6 CUPS (48 FL OZ/1.4 L)

¼ cup (2 fl oz/60 ml) extra-virgin olive oil

1 large yellow onion, coarsely chopped

1 large carrot, coarsely chopped

1 large fennel bulb, coarsely chopped

3 celery stalks, coarsely chopped

Kosher salt

2 cups (16 fl oz/475 ml) dry white wine

4 cups (32 fl oz/950 ml) chicken stock

4 lb (1.8 kg) fish bones, heads, and bodies, or fish and shellfish

3 star anise pods

2 bay leaves

2 teaspoons black peppercorns

4 fresh thyme sprigs

In an 8-qt (7.6-l) stockpot over medium-high heat, warm the oil. Add the onion, carrot, fennel, and celery and cook, stirring occasionally, until softened and starting to brown, about 10 minutes. Season with a big pinch of salt.

Reduce the heat to medium-low and add the wine, stirring to scrape up the browned bits. Add the chicken stock; fish bones, heads, and bodies; star anise pods; bay leaves; peppercorns; and thyme sprigs. Add enough water to cover the ingredients, about 2 cups (16 fl oz/475 ml). Increase the heat to medium-high and bring to a vigorous simmer for 1 minute. Reduce the heat, cover, and simmer gently, stirring occasionally, for about 2 hours.

Strain the stock through a fine-mesh sieve into a large bowl and skim off the fat if desired. Taste and adjust the seasoning with salt; the stock should be briny and pleasantly salty. Use immediately, refrigerate up to 3 days, or freeze for up to 3 months.

BELLE'S POMODORO SAUCE

MAKES ABOUT 3 CUPS (24 FL OZ/700 ML)

2 cans (each 28 oz/800 g) whole San Marzano tomatoes with juices

¾ cup (6 oz/170 g) unsalted butter, cut into 6 pieces

1 yellow onion, halved lengthwise with stem intact

3 cloves garlic, smashed

1 piece Parmesan cheese rind, about 3 inches (7.5 cm) square

Kosher salt

In a large, deep frying pan or saucepan over medium heat, combine the tomatoes and their juices, butter, onion halves, garlic, Parmesan rind, and 2 teaspoons salt. Bring to a simmer and cook, uncovered, stirring occasionally and crushing the tomatoes as they cook down, until the tomatoes are mostly crushed and the sauce is reduced slightly, 1–1½ hours. Remove the pan from the heat and discard the onion and Parmesan rind.

Let the sauce cool slightly, then transfer to a blender and blend until smooth, about 1 minute. The sauce can be made up to 4 days in advance; let cool completely, then refrigerate in an airtight container until ready to use.

HOMEMADE PIZZA DOUGH

MAKES 1 LB (450 G) DOUGH

1 tablespoon active dry yeast

1 teaspoon sugar

1 cup (8 fl oz/240 ml) warm water
(105°–115°F/40–46°C)

3 cups (12¾ oz/360 g) all-purpose flour

1 teaspoon kosher salt

2 tablespoons extra-virgin olive oil

In a small bowl, dissolve the yeast and sugar in the warm water and let stand until foamy, about 5 minutes.

In the bowl of a food processor fitted with the dough blade, combine the flour and salt and pulse 4 times to mix. With the motor running on the dough speed, slowly add the yeast mixture, allowing each addition to be absorbed before adding more. Continue processing until the dough forms a ball and cleans the sides of the bowl, about 1 minute, then process for 1 minute more.

Coat the inside of a large bowl with the oil and place the dough in the bowl. Cover with a damp kitchen towel and let the dough rise in a warm place until doubled in size, about 1½ hours. Use as directed in individual recipes. To store the dough for later use, skip the rise. Cover the bowl with plastic wrap and refrigerate for up to 3 days, or wrap the dough in plastic wrap and freeze for up to 3 months, then thaw in the refrigerator. Bring to room temperature before using.

WHITE SAUCE

MAKES ABOUT 1 CUP (8 FL OZ/240 ML)

3 tablespoons unsalted butter

3 tablespoons all-purpose flour

1¼ cups (10 fl oz/300 ml) whole milk

1 clove garlic, grated

½ cup (2 oz/60 g) grated
Parmesan cheese

Kosher salt and freshly ground pepper

In a small saucepan over medium-low heat, melt the butter. Add the flour and cook, whisking constantly to prevent lumps from forming, until a thick paste forms, 3–4 minutes. While continuing to whisk, slowly add the milk. Cook, stirring often, until the mixture is thick enough to coat the back of a spoon, about 4 minutes. Add the garlic and cheese and cook, stirring often, until the sauce reaches the consistency of a thick gravy, about 4 minutes longer. Reduce the heat to low if the sauce starts to scorch. Season to taste with salt and pepper. Remove from the heat and use right away, or let cool, transfer to an airtight container, and refrigerate for up to 3 days.

SHALLOT-DIJON VINAIGRETTE

MAKES 1¼ CUPS (10 FL OZ/300 ML)

½ cup (4 fl oz/120 ml) extra-virgin olive oil

2 shallots, thinly sliced

Kosher salt and freshly ground pepper

2 cloves garlic

⅓ cup (2¾ fl oz/80 ml) red wine vinegar

1 tablespoon Dijon mustard

1 tablespoon honey, preferably local wildflower honey

Set a small, fine-mesh sieve over a 2-cup (16–fl oz/475-ml) heatproof measuring cup. Line a small baking sheet with paper towels. In a medium frying pan over medium-low heat, heat the oil until hot. Add the shallots and cook, stirring, until golden brown, about 15 minutes.

Carefully pour the shallots and hot oil into the sieve; let cool for 5 minutes. Transfer the shallots to the prepared baking sheet and lightly season with salt. (Use the shallots with the vinaigrette in a recipe or save for another use, such as topping the bistro-style salad on page 51. Or just eat them off the pan like we do in the Test Kitchen!)

Finely grate the garlic into the shallot oil. Whisk to combine. In another bowl, whisk together the vinegar, mustard, and honey. Season with 1 teaspoon salt and ¼ teaspoon pepper. While whisking, add the garlic-shallot oil in a slow, steady stream, continuing to whisk until emulsified. Taste and adjust the seasoning with salt. Use immediately, or refrigerate in an airtight container for up to 2 weeks.

GRANCH DIP

MAKES ABOUT 1½ CUPS (12 FL OZ/350 ML)

1½ cups (12 oz/340 g) plain Greek yogurt

¼ cup (½ oz/15 g) chopped fresh chives

1 tablespoon finely chopped fresh dill

1 tablespoon finely chopped fresh flat-leaf parsley leaves

2 tablespoons fresh lemon juice

1½ teaspoons granulated garlic

Kosher salt and freshly ground pepper

In a bowl, combine the yogurt, chives, dill, parsley, lemon juice, and granulated garlic and stir to mix well. Season with salt and pepper. The dip can be stored in an airtight container in the refrigerator for up to 1 week.

DIJONNAISE DIP

MAKES ABOUT 1½ CUPS (12 FL OZ/350 ML)

1 cup (8 fl oz/240 ml) mayonnaise

2 tablespoons Dijon mustard

1 tablespoon whole-grain mustard

1 teaspoon fresh lemon juice

Kosher salt

In a bowl, combine the mayonnaise, both mustards, and lemon juice and stir to mix well. Season with salt. The dip can be stored in an airtight container in the refrigerator for up to 1 week.

NOT-SO-SECRET SAUCE

MAKES ABOUT 1½ CUPS (12 FL OZ/350 ML)

½ cup (4 oz/115 g) ketchup

½ cup (4 fl oz/120 ml) mayonnaise

2 tablespoons yellow mustard

2 tablespoons barbecue sauce

Kosher salt

In a bowl, combine the ketchup, mayonnaise, mustard, and barbecue sauce and stir to mix well. Season with salt. The sauce can be stored in an airtight container in the refrigerator for up to 1 week.

HOT HONEY

MAKES ABOUT ⅔ CUP (8 OZ/225 G)

1 cup (12 oz/340 g) honey,
preferably local wildflower honey

1 tablespoon red pepper flakes

½ teaspoon kosher salt

1 tablespoon apple cider vinegar

1–2 large jalapeño chiles, sliced into
rounds ⅛ inch (3 mm) thick (see Tip)

In a small saucepan over medium heat, combine the honey and red pepper flakes and simmer, stirring occasionally, about 3 minutes. Remove from the heat and stir in the salt and apple cider vinegar. Allow the mixture to cool slightly, about 5 minutes, then add the jalapeños. Let the mixture infuse for about 30 minutes, then strain the mixture through a fine-mesh sieve set over a heatproof bowl. Transfer the jalapeños to a separate bowl and set aside.

Return the infused honey to the saucepan over medium-low heat and simmer for about 3 minutes. The honey may boil and rise; if so, remove from the heat and allow the honey to cool and thicken, about 30 minutes. Serve immediately with the reserved jalapeños, if desired, or transfer to an airtight container and refrigerate for up to 3 days.

TIP Before you slice it, take a small bite of the jalapeño to gauge the heat level. If it's spicy, use 1 chile; if it's light on heat, use 2 chiles.

PICKLED RED ONION

MAKES ABOUT 1½ CUPS (6 OZ/170 G)

1 large red onion, very thinly sliced

¾ cup (6 fl oz/180 ml) apple cider vinegar or white wine vinegar

¼ cup (2 fl oz/60 ml) water

1 teaspoon honey, preferably local wildflower honey, or sugar

Kosher salt

Place the onion slices in a heatproof jar or bowl. In a small saucepan over medium-high heat, combine the vinegar, water, honey, and 1 teaspoon salt. Bring to a simmer for 1 minute.

Pour the vinegar mixture over the onion slices, submerging them completely in the liquid. Cover and refrigerate for at least 1 hour or up to 2 weeks.

OLIVE-JALAPEÑO SALSA VERDE

MAKES ABOUT 1½ CUPS (12 FL OZ/350 ML)

½ cup (2 oz/60 g) pitted Castelvetrano olives, minced

1 bunch green onions, white and light green parts, finely chopped

½ bunch fresh flat-leaf parsley, leaves and tender stems only, minced

1 jalapeño chile, seeded (optional) and minced

1 tablespoon finely grated lemon zest

1 clove garlic, minced

1 cup (8 fl oz/240 ml) extra-virgin olive oil

2 tablespoons white wine vinegar or champagne vinegar

Kosher salt and freshly ground pepper

In a bowl, combine the olives, green onions, parsley, jalapeño, lemon zest, and garlic. Add the oil, vinegar, and salt and pepper to taste and stir to combine. Serve immediately, or transfer to an airtight container and refrigerate for up to 1 week.

LENA'S CHILI CRISP

MAKES ABOUT 1 CUP (8 OZ)

**FOR THE SHALLOT AND
GARLIC CRISPS**

3 medium shallots

6 large cloves garlic

1 cup (8 fl oz/240 ml) neutral oil,
such as avocado

2 green onions, white and
green parts separated

3-inch (7.5-cm) piece fresh ginger,
peeled and halved lengthwise

2 orange peel strips, each 3–4 inches
(7.5–10 cm) long, preferably Valencia

1 tablespoon Sichuan peppercorns

2 star anise pods

1 cinnamon stick

1 bay leaf

FOR THE POUR-OVER INGREDIENTS

5 tablespoons (scant 1 oz/25 g)
gochugaru (Korean pepper flakes)

3 tablespoons red pepper flakes

1 tablespoon sugar

2 teaspoons mushroom bouillon powder

1 teaspoon salt

1 teaspoon tamari or low-sodium
soy sauce

To make the shallot and garlic crisps, using a mandoline, thinly slice the shallots crosswise into rings and the garlic cloves lengthwise, preferably no more than $\frac{1}{16}$ inch (2 mm) thick. Set aside.

Set a fine-mesh sieve over a heatproof bowl with a pouring spout or a large (4-cup/32-fl oz/950-ml) glass measuring cup; set aside. Line a rimmed baking sheet with paper towels and set aside.

In a 4-qt (3.7-l) saucepan, heat the oil over medium-high heat for 2 minutes. Add the shallots (they will begin to sizzle), reduce the heat to medium-low, and simmer, stirring continuously around the edges of the saucepan with wooden chopsticks or a wooden spoon, until light golden brown, 6–10 minutes. Immediately pour the shallots and oil into the fine-mesh sieve. Drain the shallots thoroughly, then transfer them to the prepared baking sheet, spreading them out so they don't stick together as they cool. Return the oil to the saucepan and return the sieve to over the bowl.

Return the pan to medium heat and warm the oil. Add the sliced garlic. When it begins to sizzle, reduce the heat to medium-low and fry, stirring occasionally, until medium golden brown, about 3 minutes.

Immediately pour the garlic and oil into the fine-mesh sieve. Scatter the garlic next to the fried shallot on the prepared baking sheet. Return the oil to the saucepan and return the sieve to over the bowl.

Return the pan to medium heat and warm the oil. Add the green onions, ginger, orange peels, Sichuan peppercorns, star anise pods, cinnamon stick, and bay leaf. Once the aromatics begin to sizzle, reduce the heat to low and simmer, stirring occasionally, to infuse for 30 minutes; watch carefully and adjust the heat to maintain a gentle simmer. If any of the ingredients begin to burn (such as the orange peel or green part of the green onions), remove those ingredients and continue simmering.

Meanwhile, to prepare the pour-over ingredients, in a medium heatproof bowl, combine the gochugaru, red pepper flakes, sugar, mushroom bouillon powder, and salt.

When the aromatics have finished simmering, pour the contents of the pan into the fine-mesh sieve, then discard the contents of the sieve. Let the oil cool to 280°F (138°C) on an instant-read thermometer. If the oil is not warm enough, return it to the saucepan and heat gently. Pour the oil over the gochugaru mixture and stir to combine. Let stand for 15 minutes to allow the ingredients to infuse.

Meanwhile, finely crush 2 tablespoons of the fried garlic with the flat bottom of a measuring cup. Transfer to a bowl and add 2 tablespoons uncrushed garlic. Finely crush ¼ cup (¾ oz/25 g) of the fried shallots and combine with the garlic. (The remaining fried garlic and shallots can be stored in an airtight container at room temperature for up to 1 week.)

Stir the tamari into the gochugaru-oil mixture, then add the garlic-shallot mixture and stir again. Transfer to an airtight jar and store at room temperature for up to 1 month. Serve on anything and everything.

TIP **This condiment includes a mixture of Lena's favorite aromatics paired with two variations of chili flakes—the red pepper flakes commonly seen in grocery stores and Korean gochugaru, which adds more sweetness and a slightly smoky and more peppery flavor. Look for gochugaru in Asian markets or online. This recipe yields more fried shallots and garlic than you need to make the chili crisp. Use the extra to garnish your favorite dishes. We like to add them to The Test Kitchen Chopped Salad on page 81.**

LEMON AIOLI

MAKES ABOUT 1 CUP (8 FL OZ/240 ML)

1 clove garlic

Kosher salt

1 large egg plus 1 large egg yolk

1 cup (8 fl oz/240 ml) neutral oil,
such as canola

Finely grated zest and juice of ½ lemon

In a blender or small food processor, combine the garlic and a big pinch of salt and pulse several times until the garlic is minced. Add the whole egg and egg yolk and pulse to combine. With the machine running, slowly add a few drops of the oil and then follow with a slow, steady stream of oil. Continue to blend until thoroughly combined. Transfer to a bowl, then stir in the lemon zest and juice. Taste and adjust the seasoning with salt. The aioli can be covered and refrigerated for up to 3 days.

VARIATIONS

Dijon Aioli: Add 1 tablespoon each Dijon mustard and whole-grain mustard with the egg and egg yolk.

Meyer Lemon Aioli: Use the finely grated zest and juice of 1 Meyer lemon for the lemon zest and juice.

Garlic Aioli: Omit the lemon zest. Increase the garlic to 3 cloves.

BASIL PESTO

MAKES ABOUT 1 CUP (8 OZ)

½ cup (2 oz/60 g) packed grated
Parmesan cheese

¼ cup (1¼ oz/35 g) toasted pine nuts,
walnuts, or almonds

3 cups (3 oz/90 g) fresh basil leaves

1 cup (8 fl oz/240 ml) extra-virgin
olive oil

Kosher salt and freshly ground pepper

In a food processor, combine the Parmesan and pine nuts and process until finely ground. Add the basil and pulse until finely chopped. With the processor running, pour in ¾ cup (6 fl oz/180 ml) of the oil and process until blended, then stir in the remaining ¼ cup (2 fl oz/60 ml) oil. The pesto will be slightly loose and oily. Season to taste with salt and pepper. The pesto can be made up to 4 days in advance; cover and refrigerate until ready to use. Bring to room temperature before serving.

CHERMOULA

MAKES 1½ CUPS (12 FL OZ/350 ML)

4 cloves garlic

2 bunches fresh cilantro, leaves and tender stems only

1 bunch fresh flat-leaf parsley, leaves and tender stems only

1 tablespoon ground cumin

2 teaspoons ground coriander

2 teaspoons red pepper flakes

1 teaspoon sweet paprika

Juice of 1 lemon

Kosher salt and freshly ground black pepper

1 cup (8 fl oz/240 ml) extra-virgin olive oil

With a food processor running, drop the garlic through the feed tube and process until minced. Stop the processor and scrape down the sides of the bowl. Working in batches, add the cilantro and parsley and pulse until coarsely chopped. Add the cumin, coriander, red pepper flakes, paprika, lemon juice, 1 teaspoon salt, and ½ teaspoon black pepper and pulse until combined. With the processor running, slowly pour in the oil and process until a smooth sauce forms. Taste and adjust the seasoning with salt and black pepper if needed. Use immediately or refrigerate in an airtight container for up to 1 week.

SIMPLE SYRUP

MAKES ABOUT 1½ CUPS (12 FL OZ/350 ML)

1 cup (8 fl oz/240 ml) water

1 cup (7 oz/200 g) sugar

In a small saucepan over medium-high heat, bring the water to a simmer. Add the sugar and stir until it completely dissolves. Remove the pan from the heat and set aside to cool to room temperature. Refrigerate in an airtight container until ready to use, up to 1 month.

WHIPPED CREAM

MAKES ABOUT 2 CUPS (16 FL OZ/475 ML)

1 cup (8 fl oz/240 ml) heavy cream

2 tablespoons sugar

1 teaspoon pure vanilla extract

In a bowl, using an electric mixer, beat together the cream, sugar, and vanilla on medium-high speed until soft-to-medium peaks form. Serve immediately, or cover and refrigerate until ready to serve. Briefly beat the cream again with a whisk if there is any separation.

INDEX

BIOS

Belle English is the director and head chef of the Williams Sonoma Test Kitchen, where she oversees all recipe development, product testing, cookbook creation, and culinary content. Born and raised in Boston, Belle fell in love with cooking and baking at an early age in her family's restaurants and opened a bakery of her own when she was just seventeen. She has spent her entire career working in professional kitchens, editorial test kitchens, and in her own kitchen running a catering company. A resident of San Francisco, Belle is also a writer, culinary illustrator, and food stylist.

Devon Francis is a chef in the Williams Sonoma Test Kitchen, where she develops recipes and oversees product testing. Born and raised in Los Angeles, she grew up eating locally grown ingredients and cooking meals inspired by her family's Italian heritage. However, cooking health-focused dishes and seeing the positive impact, is what ultimately led her to attend San Francisco Cooking School. Devon can be found walking or running with friends throughout the city, exploring the latest health trends, and happily eating her way through it all.

Lena Wu is a chef in the Williams Sonoma Test Kitchen, where she specializes in food product and recipe development. As a first-generation Chinese American with parents raised in Korea, Lena draws inspiration from the rich culinary traditions of both cultures. She began her culinary education in the kitchen of her family's restaurant in Berkeley, California, and later attended San Francisco Cooking School. Lena loves savoring spicy, global flavors, drinking wine, and exploring new cities.

AT HOME FAVORITES: 110+ RECIPES FROM THE TEST KITCHEN

Conceived and produced by Weldon Owen International
in collaboration with Williams Sonoma, Inc.
3250 Van Ness Avenue, San Francisco, CA 94109

A Weldon Owen Production
PO Box 3088
San Rafael, CA 94912
www.weldonowen.com

weldon**owen**

CEO Raoul Goff
Publisher Roger Shaw
Associate Publisher Amy Marr
Editorial Director Katie Killebrew
Assistant Editor Jourdan Plautz
VP of Creative Chrissy Kwasnik
Design Manager Megan Sinead Bingham
Production Designer Jean Hwang
Production Manager Josh Smith

Designer Ali Zeigler
Photographer Erin Scott
Food Stylist Lillian Kang
Prop Stylist Emma Star Jensen

Library of Congress Cataloging-in-Publication data
is available.

ISBN: 978-1-68188-781-4

Manufactured in China by Insight Editions
10 9 8 7 6 5 4 3 2 1

Weldon Owen wishes to thank the following people for their generous support in producing
this book: Kim Laidlaw, Rachel Markowitz, Elizabeth Parson, and Sharon Silva.

Insight Editions, in association with Roots of Peace, will plant two trees for each tree used in
the manufacturing of this book. Roots of Peace is an internationally renowned humanitarian
organization dedicated to eradicating land mines worldwide and converting war-torn lands into
productive farms and wildlife habitats. Roots of Peace will plant two million fruit and nut trees
in Afghanistan and provide farmers there with the skills and support necessary for sustainable
land use.